The White Gull Inn
More Favorite Recipes From Our Kitchen
CENTENNIAL COOKBOOK

DOOR COUNTY

Edited
by Andy Coulson

Copyright © 1997 by Andy and Jan Coulson

First Edition

ISBN Number 0-942495-74-8

Library of Congress 97-073879

Printed in the United States of America by
Palmer Publications, Inc.
PO Box 296
318 North Main Street
Amherst, Wisconsin 54406

Designed by Amherst Press
a division of Palmer Publications, Inc.

Cover photo and other color photography
by Bill Paulson unless otherwise credited

Black and white photographs of early Fish Creek courtesy of
Gibraltar Historical Association

For copies of this book or
Favorite Recipes From Our Kitchen: The White Gull Inn contact
The White Gull Inn
PO Box 160
Fish Creek, Wisconsin 54212

or

Amherst Press
PO Box 296
Amherst, Wisconsin 54406

CONTENTS

Acknowledgments v

Dedication vi

Door County Fish Boil vii

Introduction 1

History of the White Gull Inn 3

The White Gull Inn Today 12

Door County Seasons 14

Recipes

Breakfast & Brunch 19

Breads 31

Soups 39

Dressings 55

Salads & Side Dishes 61

Sandwiches 77

Appetizers 83

Entrees 91

Desserts 107

Index 133

The White Gull Inn on a summer day.

ACKNOWLEDGMENTS

In the preface to our first cookbook, published in 1990, I gave credit to the many cooks and staff members who had worked on that project. A cookbook, I noted, is not unlike a special candlelight dinner. Just as the chef, baker, prep cooks, waitresses and host all contribute to one's ultimate enjoyment of a meal, many staff members were involved in the process of translating popular White Gull breakfast, lunch and dinner items into a collection of easy to follow recipes.

Seven years later, as we wrap up the work on our second cookbook, I am amazed at how many of the same people are involved, a testament to what a low staff turnover the White Gull has been lucky to have. We believe there is a connection between low turnover and consistency of quality in any enterprise, especially a restaurant, and Jan and I feel most fortunate to be thanking these same staff members: Chef John Vreeke, who presides over the White Gull's candlelight dinners, and kitchen manager Julie Zak, who presides over breakfasts and lunches; bakers Steve Glabe and Gregg Steffen and sous-chef Dean Pahl were already veteran staff members in 1990, as was Scott Kositzke, who doubles as kitchen manager on Julie's day off, then moves to managing the "front of the house" for the rest of the week. Thanks also to baker Mary Lemens who has joined our staff since the first cookbook was published. Not only are the above responsible for creating, testing and refining recipes, but they are also charged with using their own and others' recipes day after day to create memorable meals for our guests. And thanks also to the many other staff members, past and present, who have played such an important role in making the White Gull such a special place.

Although she has recently left our staff, we'd like to thank Laurel Hauser for once again editing and testing recipes, and nudging along the rest of us when we became distracted with other day to day responsibilities.

White Gull Inn chef John Vreeke presents Oriental Pan-Seared Sea Scallops.

DEDICATION

A friend we're not able to thank personally, but who is never far from our thoughts, is Russ Ostrand, the White Gull's master fish boiler for more than 30 years, who passed away in April of 1997. Not only did Russ provide a special experience for thousands of Door County visitors, but he was a wonderful role model for all of us mentioned here and for generations of young people who worked a summer or two at the White Gull Inn. Jan and I are pleased to dedicate this cookbook in his memory.

Harmann's Studio photo

DOOR COUNTY FISH BOIL

It is dusk in Fish Creek, and a gusty wind whips a few leaves about the patio. The dinner guests at the White Gull Inn don't seem to mind the falling temperatures. They are all outside, standing around a huge black pot filled with boiling water and suspended over a blazing wood fire. Clutching mugs of beer and cider, they draw close to the flames, keeping warm and straining to hear the man who appears to be skimming the pot and giving a short course in cooking.

Some of the guests are locals entertaining out of town visitors. The rest are tourists, experiencing something everyone has heard about from the moment they set foot on the Door Peninsula—a traditional outdoor fish boil. The master boiler explains the history of the fish boil and the unusual cooking procedure, then patiently answers questions.

"How did the fish boil get started?" asks one guest. Tom Schneider, the boiler, begins the answer as though he has never heard the question before.

"Well, people have been boiling fish for thousands of years. I don't know who did it first in Door County. Maybe the commercial fishermen who had access to lots of fish, and wanted a quick and easy meal. Churches picked up the tradition to raise money, and people from all over would come to taste the

White Gull Inn fish boil.

Harmann's Studio photo

Early Fish Creek commercial fishermen collecting herring from their nets.

local fish, potatoes and Door County cherry pie. Eventually the restaurants got into the act."

Tom now adds the salt, something which never fails to catch the crowd's attention because of the amount used in the fish boil recipe—one pound for every two gallons of water. "Is that salt?" someone gasps. "Just a pinch," answers Tom. Then with a smile forming on his face, red from the heat, he explains, "the salt does not make the fish and potatoes salty. It raises the specific gravity of the water, and makes everything float. The fish oils that we don't want to eat rise to the surface. When the fish and potatoes are cooked, I throw on the kerosene."

At this point, someone invariably asks if the kerosene goes into the pot itself. Because boiled fish doesn't sound too appealing to begin with—until you've tried it—Tom stresses that the kerosene goes on the fire only. The big flare-up, he explains, causes the overboil, when the water in the top half of the pot boils over the edge, taking the oils with it.

Tom measures that "small amount of kerosene" into an old coffee can. You can tell those who've been here before because they move back, forming a wide ring around the fire and the boiler. For the newcomers, Tom warns them to give the fire plenty of room. "You don't want an immovable object right behind you if the wind shifts," he advises. With the crowd at a respectful distance and his assistant behind him, ready with a long pole, Tom tosses the kerosene on the flames. A wall of fire shoots skyward, water pours over the side of the pot, hissing as it hits the coals. A dozen camera flashes go off, as the assistant and Tom ease the pole through the nets of fish and potatoes and lift them gently out to set on a nearby tray.

Tom peers through the steam into the net as though checking to see if the fish is properly cooked. That it wouldn't be is hard to fathom, since Tom by now has cooked thousands of fish boil dinners. He raises his head and smiles incredulously at his assistant. "It looks good enough to eat!"

Inside the dining room, the dinner guests devour the fish and potatoes, doused in melted butter and served with the traditional accompaniments of coleslaw, rye bread and cherry pie. Waitresses bustle in and out of the kitchen with seconds and glasses of Wisconsin beer. As people enjoy their dinner, the noise level of the dining room gradually rises until a piece of cherry pie with a candle is set down in front of some lucky guest. The waitress leads eighty voices in a rousing "Happy Birthday."

Before the singing stops, Tom is already back outside, ringing the black kettle with fresh firewood and getting the water back to a boil. As he pours five pounds of salt into the pot, someone asks, "Is that salt?" "I hope so," says Tom, with a grin.

Tom learned to boil fish from the same man I did—Russ Ostrand, who for 30 years was the White Gull Inn's master fish boiler. Russ passed away in early 1997, but he is remembered fondly by generations of tourists and staff members as the dean of Door County fish boilers. Even if you never attended one of his fish boil dinners, you may have seen his picture in one of the many regional and national magazines and newspapers that featured him.

In 1972, when I became the owner and manager of the White Gull Inn, I was young and green, and had no real idea of how to run a business, let alone a Door County fish boil. Someone said to call Russ, who had been the inn's fish boiler for the last few years. "Well," I remember him saying when I called and introduced myself. "I heard the White Gull had been sold, so I have been asked to boil fish for another restaurant."

In the stunned silence that followed, he must have taken pity on me, for he finally said, "but I would like to stay at the White Gull."

Russ was a Door County native, who along with boiling fish, farmed and worked as a pipe fitter at Peterson Shipyards in Sturgeon Bay. In the beginning, he had to teach me and my new staff everything, for we knew nothing. That first weekend we were open, Russ calmly boiled the fish and entertained the dinner guests with his accordion. Behind the scenes he patiently explained to us where to buy the fish, how to build the fire, how to count out the servings, where to stand, what to say, even how to clean up. I often have wondered what he was thinking as he drove home each night that first summer. But it was obvious that he took an interest in young people, and he wasn't about to let anything bad happen to the inn he took great pride in.

Eventually, Russ taught me, Tom and a few others to boil the fish, so he could take an occasional evening off. Upon returning, he would question us carefully to make sure that everything had gone all right. Russ and I had worked enough boils together to know that things don't always go as planned. Like the time in 1972 when the serving table collapsed and the lemon bread spilled all over the floor, covered with tartar sauce. You could hear a pin drop until Russ broke the silence with, "Anyone know any good jokes?" Everyone cracked up and Russ broke into a tune on his accordion while the staff righted the table and brought out fresh food.

Then there was the night a bat flew through the lobby, and fifty people hit the deck. Or the time when Russ's assistant dropped a whole net of cooked fish on the patio. It wouldn't have been so bad, but there wasn't enough fish left in the cooler to feed the crowd. Russ calmly boiled what was on hand while I ran down the street to borrow fish from a competitor. By the time the first batch was cooked, I had made it back with just enough for the rest, and the show went on.

Once, back in the days when people used to eat out on the patio in summer, a line squall moved through. Everyone grabbed their food and dashed for cover, as the staff went through its storm drill of moving in tables and chairs. After everyone was situated, a staff member looked out the window to discover that someone had forgotten a baby out in the rain. Nowadays, that couldn't happen, as everyone eats inside, rain or shine. The only two people that have to be outside are the boiler and his assistant.

Russ encouraged me to play my banjo when I boiled, and once or twice asked me to accompany him while he played the accordion. What the dinner guests thought of sitting down to a dinner of boiled fish while a bluegrass banjo player and button accordionist tried to play German polkas is hard to fathom, but we sure had a lot of fun.

If that first summer of 1972 was a crash course for us in fish boiling, it was only kindergarten in the school of Russ Ostrand. My staff and I were young, and most of us had come to Door County on a lark or just to have fun while earning money for college. As we watched our fish boiling mentor, we realized that although he was enjoying himself too, there was a whole lot more going on. Sure, there were polkas, and singing, and clapping, and yes, even sometimes dancing at the fish boils. But something else was happening: Russ was taking this very seriously. Sure, he'd tell a few jokes and put the guests at ease. But he was scrupulous about how he cooked the fish. He carefully and kindly answered every question, no matter how many times he'd been asked it. It became obvious that he loved the fish boil, was proud of it, wanted to share it with others, and took great pains to make sure that everyone's visit to his fish boil, whether it was a first or a repeat, was a very special experience. It was this way of approaching what you do, every day, with your best effort, in order to make it special for other people, that Russ passed on to me and Tom and to the others he worked with.

Russ was a modest person, but he was actually quite famous. Not too many of us can say that our picture has appeared in the *New York Times, Chicago Tribune, Better Homes and Gardens, Country Living*…the list goes on and on, including a lot of television stations. We lost track of the number long ago. But all this media attention never went to Russ's head. What was far more important to him were the thousands of people who planned their annual vacation around a visit to his fish boil. He looked forward to seeing them each year as much as they did to seeing him.

Russ is gone now, but he lives on in our memories and his tradition is passed on at each fish boil by Tom, me and others who were lucky enough to learn from him.

Harmann's Studio photo

(See page 98 for the White Gull Inn Fish Boil recipe.)

Harmann's Studio photo

Winter at the White Gull Inn.

INTRODUCTION

Recipes were not always shared at the White Gull Inn. In fact, when we became innkeepers in 1972, what few we could find were kept under lock and key. At that time, the White Gull was not serving any meal except the Door County fish boil, so few recipes were needed.

When we became comfortable with the fish boils, which were served only four evenings a week, we began to introduce the other meals that the previous management had abandoned. First came the breakfasts, which, we reasoned, were a necessity for a country inn. Then came lunches and finally, we brought back the Early American Buffet, a meal the inn had been famous for many years before. Our Early American Buffet combined recipes from the previous owners and ones Jan had collected from friends and family members. It took a while for the public to rediscover our restaurant, but those who came enthusiastically encouraged our efforts. It wasn't long before we received our first recipe request. For a time, we obliged by scribbling down recipes on the nearest piece of paper.

Eventually, the requests came so regularly that we conceived our first cookbook project. Selection of recipes was the easy part—they were the ones most often requested. Getting them broken down into smaller servings, then down onto paper, tested and re-tested, was time consuming. That project took several years to reach fruition, always being pushed to the back burner when some more pressing issue or challenge presented itself. Eventually, we made it our number one priority, and in 1990, *Favorite Recipes From Our Kitchen: The White Gull Inn* was published.

We relaxed, but not for long. Our talented chefs never stop creating and experimenting, and soon we were being besieged with requests for recipes not in the cookbook. Thus began work on our second cookbook. It has been seven years in the making, and we think you'll be pleased with this collection of *More Favorite Recipes From Our Kitchen.*

A family portrait of White Gull Inn founder
Dr. Herman Welcker, his wife Henriette,
and only daughter Mathilda.

HISTORY OF THE WHITE GULL INN

It could be a story from the nineteen seventies or eighties: a middle-aged professional gives up his lucrative practice and moves to a remote village to become an innkeeper. Except that it happened in 1896.

In the 1890s, Fish Creek, on Wisconsin's Door Peninsula, was a bustling little town that was changing from a fishing community to a summer tourist village. It lacked electricity, telephones and automobiles, and overland access was limited to a rough-and-tumble stage ride from Sturgeon Bay. However, visitors so appreciated the cool air and peaceful beauty that they were willing to make the trip each summer on the Goodrich Steam Line from cities around Lake Michigan. One resort, already established, was operated by Asa Thorp, founder of the hamlet.

Enter Dr. Herman Welcker, German born and educated, who at the age of 45 had emigrated to Milwaukee with his wife and daughter. In just two years, Welcker, a virologist, had apparently established an excellent reputation and practice in his adopted city. Then, on a visit to Fish Creek, his life and career would take another twist. Falling in love with the tiny village, Welcker must have realized that if he was going to support his family in Fish Creek he would have to create a business. He purchased land from Asa Thorp and constructed what is now the White Gull Inn, naming it after his wife, Henriette.

Welcker surrounded his inn with cottages and purchased more land around the village, including dock space, a farm to produce food for the inn and property which would later become Welcker's Point in Peninsula State Park. His most unusual project was moving the Lumberman's Hotel from Marinette, Wisconsin, to Fish Creek in 1907. The hotel (now known as the Whistling Swan) must have been dismantled before being moved the approximately

An early view of Fish Creek and the harbor.

Summer visitors arriving by steamer, circa 1910.

eighteen miles across the frozen waters of Green Bay. Locating his new hotel one block east of the Henriette, Welcker named it Welcker's Casino, because of the card and game tables he provided for men in the basement.

Across the street from the Casino, Dr. Welcker constructed a kitchen and dining hall, where all his guests enjoyed three hearty meals a day. He filled his inns and twelve cottages with only the finest of furnishings—walnut dressers with marble tops, oak and iron beds and a baby grand piano, at which Henriette entertained the guests. All had to be shipped in by steamer from cities as far away as Cincinnati.

What was it like to be a guest of Dr. Welcker's? Fish Creek historian Ann Thorp, who researched "Herr Doktor," describes him as:

> ...a strict disciplinarian, health and fitness enthusiast, gourmet, lover of art, music and nature; vigorous, stubborn, domineering, frugal, snobbish.

> The Doctor presided over his exclusive realm with great pride and a firm hand. An early guest once saw his portly, bearded figure standing on the porch of the Casino, gazing over his resort, and announcing "Das ist alles mein!" (This is all mine!)

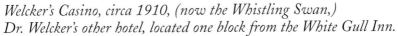

His early guests were often German friends from Milwaukee, people of "refinement," perhaps hand-chosen by Welcker. They arrived by steamer, a rigorous trip then, and stayed for the season. The doctor reserved the right to refuse rooms on whatever basis he chose: attire, personality, or attitude. One story claims that he turned away a young member of the Pabst family and his party because of their racy and outlandish clothes and rather forward manner.

He designed his program in the manner of European health spas of that era. He believed in exercise, hearty meals, rest, and cultural stimulation. A day's schedule might have begun with a hike along the shore to Ephraim, stopping at one of the little rest areas named for trees in the vicinity; there was a "Birch Bench," a "Balsam Bench," and others, with water fountains nearby. After returning by boat, perhaps the "Thistle," the large noon meal was announced by a big iron bell, and everyone was required to be on time. The table was laden with huge platters of roast pork or Wiener Schnitzel, potatoes, noodles, baked cabbage and other vegetables, smoked fish, fresh bread and rich desserts such as a three-layer cherry kuchen liberally crowned with whipped cream.

A two-hour "silent" period followed and was strictly enforced. Herr Doktor strode through cottages and hallways shaking a small hand bell, call- ing "Ruhe, Ruhe!" (Quiet, quiet!)

Swimming was a favorite pastime and exercise for the Doctor and his wife Henriette, and guests were encouraged to join them for an afternoon

Welcker's Casino, circa 1910, (now the Whistling Swan,)
Dr. Welcker's other hotel, located one block from the White Gull Inn.

dip at the Bathing Beach (now the Town Beach). Bathing costumes were made of dark wool; a two piece suit for men, knee length (one rather imperious man was seen entering the water with his Phi Beta Kappa pin fastened to his bathing suit). Women wore voluminous skirts and bloomers and often a white hat pinned to their hair, creating a merry picture of white dots floating and bobbing on the water.

After another hearty meal the evenings were devoted to music, games, and socializing at the Casino. Women had a sewing room and a card room for bridge or mah-jongg. Game and billiard tables were set up in the basement for the men, and there were Ping-Pong tables and other amusements for children. There were ice boxes stocked with beer and other beverages, available on an honor system.

Plays were presented starring some of the guests or visiting actors, and concerts performed by professional musicians from Chicago and Milwaukee. The great opera singer Madame Schumann-Heinck once sang at the Casino. The great hall was hung with paintings by famous artists. Guests sometimes went to the Town Hall to see the flickery movies of that time.

At ten o'clock sharp the day was over and all the kerosene lamps were to be extinguished. Herr Doktor patrolled the walks and would shout up to a lighted window, "Abdrehen!" (Turn it off!)

Welcker had his office in his home, across from the Casino. Guests went there to pay their weekly bill and were amazed at his collection of snake skins, butterflies, antlers, a boar's head, stuffed fish, and stacks of books and sheet music.

Evidently he gave up his medical practice when he established his resort, but he would occasionally prescribe for a mild illness. He had once studied

Herman and Henriette Welcker, founders of the White Gull Inn, enjoying an afternoon dip at the Fish Creek bathing beach.

An early view of Fish Creek's Main Street.

virology, and when a smallpox epidemic threatened the village, he undertook the task of manufacturing a vaccine. At the time he didn't have the breed of cattle necessary for the production of the vaccine. Instead, he used a local boy, Merle Thorp, then about eleven years old. Merle was vaccinated over and over, and the Doctor used his blood to make vaccine for the rest of "der kinder" in the town.

Throughout the warm summer days the figure of Herr Doktor prevailed, a sometimes romantic image. There is an old photo of him on a boat trip to Chambers Island, with a lovely young lady on each arm, his bright eyes showing his pleasure and admiration. His old-world sentimentality was evident when he named the cottages for the women in his life—the Henriette, the Mathilda, the Hermine, the Tina, the Minna, and the Else.

After Henriette's death in 1920 and Herman's in 1924, Welcker's Resort was managed by a niece, Martha Fahr, until her death in 1939. Then Welcker's domain was split up, with his inns and other properties going to various owners.

The Henriette went through a succession of owners and several name changes, including Sunset Beach Guest Home and Lakewood Lodge. During the nineteen fifties and sixties, many of Door County's historic inns were either torn down or remodeled beyond recognition to accommodate the public's changing tastes in travel. Perhaps the Henriette would eventually have suffered the same fate had it not been purchased, in 1959, by a young couple from Madison.

Andy Redmann was a talented artist who could see beyond the aging facade. He and his wife Elsie changed the name to the White Gull Inn and set out to create their version of a New England-style hostelry. The Redmanns refinished the pine floors in the bedrooms, papered the walls with colorful prints, refinished much of the original furniture and acquired more antiques.

The White Gull Inn as it looked in the 1940s.
At that time it was known as Sunset Park Guest Home.

Andy's own watercolors were featured throughout the inn and cottages.

Andy turned his attention to the 1940s era dining room, which had been added after Welcker's Resort had been split up. A warm, Early American look emerged with the addition of the two-way fireplace, wainscoted walls, small paned windows and rough-sawn hemlock ceiling. As resourceful as he was artistic, Andy fashioned the colonial-style chandeliers out of funnels, copper tubing and muffin tins, soldered together and spray-painted black.

Elsie took over the kitchen, where for most of the year she did all the cooking and baking by herself. One of her creations was the Early American Buffet, which consisted of roast turkey and ham, baked beans, corn bread and homemade butter, churned by the young staff in the dining room.

The most popular meal started by the Redmanns, and one the inn is famous for today, is the traditional Door County fish boil. Until the 1950s, the meal, consisting of boiled fresh whitefish or lake trout, boiled red potatoes, rye bread and cherry pie, had enjoyed popularity in backyard and church picnics, but had not been discovered by the general public. In back of the inn, in the shade of the century old maple trees, Andy created a flagstone patio surrounded by a cedar hedge. Tables and chairs were set up for guests to watch the catch of the day prepared before them over an open fire. Andy boiled the fish, Elsie prepared the breads and pies, and an accordion player entertained the guests before and during their meal. That first year, the fish boil was held one night a week. Today, the fish boil is served four evenings a week, and guests make reservations weeks ahead, especially in summer.

The Redmanns owned the inn for five years. Afterwards they bought an old cherry orchard on the Fish Creek bluff, where they eventually established the Settlement Courtyard Inn and Shops complex.

The White Gull then underwent two more ownership changes. In 1972, Jan and I arrived, beginning an era that has lasted longer than any other owner except the Welckers. Our arrival was exciting, hectic, somewhat disorganized, and I am convinced we didn't really know what we were doing.

After graduating from the University of Wisconsin in 1968, I had worked as a reporter for 18 months before deciding to emigrate to Australia. A year and a half later, after working my way around that country, I found myself living in Perisher Valley up in the Snowy Mountains, employed as a surveyor's assistant.

I liked Australia and might still be there today, had I not received a telegram from an old college friend in May of 1972. The White Gull Inn was for sale. Would I join him and three other friends in buying it? A week later, I was in Fish Creek, learning the business and trying to ready the inn for a Memorial Day weekend opening. My bartending experience in Australia was apparently enough for my partners, as I was voted manager.

With more than a little help from our friends, my partners and I managed to clean the rooms and cottages, hire a staff and open on time. We were lucky to be as young and as inexperienced as we were, or we might not have had the courage to proceed. In 1972, Americans outside of New England had never heard of country inns, and bed and breakfast was a concept most people identified with Europe. The White Gull was a relic of a bygone era at a time when new motels and condominiums were the norm.

One of the first people I hired was 18-year-old Jan Lindsley, who had just graduated from high school in Green Bay, and moved to Door County. Growing up in a family as one of nine children probably prepared Jan for her future in innkeeping as much as anything.

Those early years were hard work, but a lot of fun, too. We tried to make up for our lack of capital and experience with enthusiasm, and somehow what began as a lark became a labor of love. We decided to restore rather than replace and look for customers who shared our love of tradition.

An innkeeper must be able to wear many hats, and in the early years Jan worked in nearly every position at the inn, including housekeeping, waitressing, hostessing, cooking and baking. I was usually at the front desk, but when I had a chance, I'd be out on the patio helping Russ Ostrand boil the fish and sometimes accompanying his accordion playing with my five-string banjo. Jan and I were married in 1975.

By the time we arrived, the White Gull kitchen had fallen into disrepair, and the only meal remaining was the fish boil. As soon as we could, we revived the breakfasts, lunches and the popular Early American Buffets. Eventually we changed the buffets to Candlelight Dinners, which are now served on the evenings when there is not a fish boil.

It seems as though the main inn and cottages have been under a never-ending remodeling and redecorating schedule. Eventually, all received new foundations, plumbing, wiring and were fully insulated for winter use. A second dining room was added in 1979, and the kitchen gradually was tripled in size and outfitted with modern equipment and a bakery. Jan redecorated the rooms and cottages with coordinating prints and fabrics, utilizing many of the original antiques as well as others we've collected. All but one of the rooms and cottages now has its own fireplace, upon the completion of another major renovation of the main inn and the Cliffhouse rooms undertaken in 1995 and 1997.

Slowly, our clientele began to grow, and our season grew from three months to six and eventually twelve. In 1977, a man named Norman Simpson came to visit. He was the author of a book called "Country Inns and Back Roads", and according to him, there were other inns like ours out there, and a growing number of people who liked to visit them. We happily accepted his invitation to be in his book, and since then have watched the country inn and bed and breakfast movement sweep the country.

The years have flown by. As we grew, we acquired two more cottages and two staff houses. After becoming the sole owners of the inn in the early 1980s, we purchased a large home about a block from the inn. Built by the first grocer of Fish Creek, the Lundberg House is now a four-bedroom guest house for the inn.

Charles Lundberg, first grocer of Fish Creek, with his wife and four daughters on the porch of what is now the White Gull Inn's Charles Lundberg House, circa 1900.

The White Gull Inn lobby. Harmann's Studio photo

In 1985, our interest in historic Fish Creek led us to purchase the original Welcker's Casino building. The Casino had also undergone a succession of different names and owners after Welcker's death. We closed what was by then known as the Proud Mary for the winter. After extensive remodeling and redecorating, we reopened it the following spring as the Whistling Swan Inn, a seven-room bed and breakfast. In what once had been the music room where the Welcker's guests enjoyed live concerts, Jan opened the elegant Whistling Swan Shop, featuring women's and girls' clothing and gifts.

For ten years, I continued to manage the White Gull while Jan held fort at the Whistling Swan. Though we loved the Swan and were happy to reunite the two sister inns under one ownership, we began to realize that operating both businesses was taking too much of our time away from our young family. In 1996, we sold the Whistling Swan to Jim and Laurie Roberts, and Jan rejoined me at the White Gull. Today, when we're not working side by side at the inn, we retreat to our home outside of Fish Creek, with our three daughters, Meredith, Emilie and Hannah.

By now, innkeeping is in our blood and it is hard to imagine being anything but the keepers of the White Gull. We continue to be in awe of a lifestyle that is anything but boring. Our days take us from one century to another, one minute winding the ancient grandfather clock in the the lobby, and in the next updating the White Gull website on the Internet. Where else, we often ask ourselves, would we get to wear the hats of cook, hotelier, decorator, restorer, landscaper, housekeeper, maintenance person, fish boiler…the list never ends?

The greatest reward of running the White Gull has been the opportunity to meet so many wonderful and interesting people. A building, after all, is just stone, mortar, wood and plaster, but it is the people—those who stay in it and those who care for it—that make it come alive and provide its history. We are lucky indeed to have made so many friends during the last 25 years, and have enough memories to last a lifetime.

THE WHITE GULL INN TODAY

Staying at the White Gull Inn today is like traveling back to the turn of the century but bringing along modern comforts. While the facades of the buildings remain unchanged and many of the original furnishings accent the rooms, much work has been done in recent years. Every building has received a new roof and foundation, new wiring, plumbing and been insulated for winter use.

As in many other older inns, the White Gull rooms come in all sizes. After a recent remodeling, all rooms now have private bathrooms, and all rooms and cottages except one have their own fireplace. Dr. Welcker's Suite, named for the founder of the inn, has a double whirlpool. Herman Welcker and his wife, Henriette, prided themselves on their good taste in furniture, and the walnut, oak or iron beds guests sleep in are often the Welckers' acquisitions (adapted for queen-size mattresses.) Over the years, many other antiques have been added, and the rooms are decorated with coordinating prints and fabrics that maintain the warm, turn-of-the-century flavor. Comfort, however, is strictly up-to-date, with air-conditioning, modern plumbing and little touches that make guests as comfortable as can be.

Room 3, Main Lodge. Guests of the White Gull are treated to complimentary coffee and a newspaper each morning, delivered to their room.

Suite 1 at the White Gull Inn is also known as Dr. Welcker's Suite.

Breakfast at the White Gull means waking up to the aromas of freshly ground coffee and coffee cake arising from the kitchen. Late sleepers appreciate that the Eggs Benedict, White Gull granola, hash browns, and cherry pancakes with real Door County maple syrup are served until noon. Lunches include hearty homemade soups, sandwiches, omelets, salads and tempting desserts from the White Gull bakery.

Entrees at the quiet, candlelit dinners feature fresh "catch-of-the-day" whitefish, and such regional favorites as roasted Wisconsin duckling and Beef Wellington. Only the freshest of produce and ingredients are used, and each meal is thoughtfully prepared to order. On nights the Candlelight Dinners are not served, the inn features its famous traditional Door County fish boil.

Historical accounts of those who grew up in or vacationed in Fish Creek as children depict a simpler time, devoid of many of the amusements children have access to today. Without electricity, there were no radios, televisions and amusement parks. However, children occupied their summers then doing many of the same things they do today: fishing off the end of the Fish Creek dock, going for a swim at the bathing beach or engaging in a simple tug-of-war with friends and siblings.

When the bay was too cold for swimming, younger children opted for playing in the creek for which the town is named. There they looked for polliwogs, fish, turtles and snakes. Others made makeshift rafts to paddle around the harbor. Local children could earn money picking cherries or working as caddies at the Peninsula Park Golf Course. For the children of wealthier families who "summered" in the homes along Cottage Row, there were picnics on the then undeveloped sand beaches of Lake Michigan, swimming and tennis lessons and trips to Wilson's Ice Cream parlor in Ephraim.

Children enjoying a game of tug-of-war with their teacher.

Originally, the White Gull Inn and most of the inns in northern Door County were only open between Memorial Day and Labor Day. This is still a popular time, for there is nearly every imaginable recreational activity, from golf to wind surfing, from hiking and biking to sailing and charter fishing. Door County's five state parks offer miles of trails to explore, and art galleries can be found in every nook and cranny. The Peninsula Players, America's oldest profes-

Cherry picking.

photo courtesy of Door County Chamber of Commerce

Sailing to the Strawberry Islands from Fish Creek.

The Edgewood Orchard Gallery, located in a restored barn on Peninsula Players Road, Fish Creek, features original works in all media by many of America's leading artists.

Buck Miller photo

Sunset over Green Bay as viewed from the bluff above Fish Creek.

Pat Frank photo

16

The Peninsula Players "Theater in a Garden", Fish Creek, is America's oldest professional summer stock theater.

sional summer stock theater, performs in Fish Creek, as do the renowned Peninsula Music Festival and American Folklore Theater. The 750-seat Door Community Auditorium features acclaimed performing artists from all over the world.

For a long time, Door County autumns were a well kept secret. However, in recent years, people from all over the Midwest have begun making annual trips to the peninsula in September and October to witness what one travel writer described as the "caviar of fall color."

Golfing at Peninsula State Park golf course, Fish Creek.

The changing color of the leaves make autumn one of the most popular times to visit Door County.

Darryl Beers photo

The village of Fish Creek as viewed across Fish Creek harbor from Peninsula State Park.

photo courtesy of John Mayberry

Winter is the peninsula's "Quiet Season," when the cedars and bluffs wear mantles of white. The only "crowds" one is likely to encounter are of deer. Guests spend their days exploring the miles of cross-country ski trails in Peninsula State Park, ice skating, snowshoeing or taking a sleigh ride from the front door of the inn. Evenings are spent before crackling fireplaces in guest rooms or the White Gull lobby.

White Gull Inn guests enjoy a winter sleigh ride through a Fish Creek orchard.

Door County's cherry blossoms welcome spring visitors to Door County.

John Robb photo

photo courtesy of Door County Chamber of Commerce

Famous Montmorency cherries ready for picking at a Fish Creek orchard.

The first sign of spring is the annual tapping of the sugar maple trees in early March, when days are sunny and warm, and temperatures still fall below freezing at night. April is most popular with sport fishermen, who descend on each harbor as the ice goes out. May is a month of greening and rejuvenation, peaking with the bursting of blossoms in Door County's many cherry and apple orchards.

To accommodate the increasing number of guests who like to visit Door County in every season, the White Gull Inn is now open every day of the year except Thanksgiving and Christmas Days.

BREAKFAST & BRUNCH

Montmorency Cherry Coffee Cake

Photo on page 71

Yield: 12 servings

Topping:
- 1 cup brown sugar
- 1 1/2 tablespoons cinnamon
- 1/2 cup chopped walnuts

Coffee cake:
- 2 cups sour cream
- 2 teaspoons baking soda
- 4 cups flour
- 1 tablespoon baking powder
- 1 cup (2 sticks) butter, softened
- 1 1/2 cups granulated sugar
- 4 eggs
- 2 teaspoons vanilla extract
- 2 cups pitted, frozen Montmorency or other tart cherries, thawed and drained

Preheat oven to 350 degrees. Spray a 13 x 9-inch baking pan with non-stick cooking spray.

To make topping, mix together brown sugar, cinnamon and walnuts in a small bowl; set aside.

Stir together sour cream and baking soda in a small bowl. In a separate bowl, mix flour and baking powder. In a medium mixing bowl, cream butter and sugar. Add eggs to creamed mixture, one at a time. Stir in vanilla and beat until fluffy. Add sour cream and flour mixtures alternately to creamed mixture; blend thoroughly.

Spread one half of batter in prepared pan and cover with cherries. Sprinkle one-third of reserved topping over cherries. Spread remaining half of batter on top and sprinkle remaining two-thirds topping evenly over cake. Bake 60-75 minutes. Cover with foil after 30 minutes if cake is browning too quickly. Test for doneness by inserting knife in center. Serve warm.

Cherry and Cream Cheese Stuffed French Toast

Photo on page 72

Yield: 4 servings

    1 loaf unsliced egg bread
    2 packages (3 ounces each) cream cheese,
          room temperature
  1/4 cup heavy whipping cream
 11/4 cups tart Montmorency cherries,
          drained, divided
    7 eggs, beaten
       Cinnamon
       Powdered sugar

Trim ends from loaf and cut bread into six 11/2-inch thick slices. Make a cut three-quarters down the middle of each slice. (Bread will appear to have two separate slices, but will be joined together at bottom.) Set aside.

In a small bowl, beat together cream cheese, whipping cream and 3/4 cup of the cherries. Spread approximately 1/4 cup of the mixture into the pocket of each slice of bread. Gently press slices together, evenly distributing filling. Dip stuffed slices into beaten egg and coat all sides. Place immediately on a lightly oiled, heated griddle and sprinkle with cinnamon. Cook over medium heat until golden brown, turning to fry second side. Remove cooked slices from griddle and place on a cutting board. Gently make a diagonal cut through each slice, forming two triangles. Arrange three triangles on individual plates. Sprinkle with powdered sugar and remaining cherries. Serve immediately with maple syrup.

Cherry Pancakes

Photo on page 71

Yield: 10 pancakes (4-5 inches each)

       1   cup flour
       3   tablespoons sugar
       1   tablespoon baking powder
     3/4   teaspoon baking soda
     1/4   teaspoon salt
       2   eggs, slightly beaten
    1¼   cups buttermilk
    2½   tablespoons melted butter
       1   cup pitted, tart Montmorency
           cherries, drained

In a medium bowl, stir together flour, sugar, baking powder, baking soda, and salt. In a separate bowl, mix eggs and buttermilk. Pour eggs and buttermilk into dry ingredients and stir just until smooth. Add melted butter to batter and stir to combine.

Grease heated griddle if necessary. Test if griddle is hot enough by sprinkling drops of water on top. If they skitter, griddle is ready. Pour about 3 tablespoons of batter from the end of a large spoon or pitcher onto the griddle. Cook pancakes until puffed and dry around the edges. Sprinkle 6 or 7 cherries over each pancake. Flip cakes and cook other side until golden brown. Remove cakes from griddle and garnish with a few cherries before serving. Serve with butter and warm Door County maple syrup.

White Gull Inn Granola

Photo on page 72

Yield: approximately 14 cups

1	cup rolled wheat flakes
1	cup shredded coconut
1	cup chopped mixed nuts or walnuts
1/2	cup sunflower seeds
1/3	cup sesame seeds
8	cups rolled oats
1	cup wheat germ
1/3	cup water
3/4	cup honey
3/4	cup vegetable oil
1/2	teaspoon vanilla extract
2	cups raisins

Preheat oven to 300 degrees.

In a large bowl, combine wheat flakes, coconut, mixed nuts, sunflower seeds, sesame seeds, oats and wheat germ.

In a separate bowl, whisk together water, honey, oil and vanilla until well mixed. Stir wet ingredients into dry until evenly distributed. Spread mixture out evenly onto 2 large cookie sheets. Bake, turning granola with pancake turner every 15 minutes, until golden brown, approximately 45 minutes. Remove from oven and allow to rest on baking sheets until completely cooled and dried, about 2 hours. Stir in raisins and store in an airtight container.

Breakfast Rice Pudding

Yield: 6 servings

4 cups cooked basmati rice
1 can (16 ounces) peaches,
    drained and coarsely chopped
1 cup pitted, frozen tart cherries,
    thawed and drained
1 cup heavy whipping cream
1/2 cup brown sugar, divided
1/4 cup rolled oats
1/4 cup shredded, sweetened coconut
1/4 cup chopped pecans
1/4 cup (1/2 stick) butter, melted

Preheat oven to 375 degrees. Spray a 11/2-quart casserole dish with non-stick cooking spray.

Combine rice, peaches, cherries, whipping cream and 1/4 cup of the brown sugar in a large bowl. Spoon mixture into prepared dish.

In a small bowl, mix remaining 1/4 cup brown sugar, rolled oats, coconut, pecans and melted butter; sprinkle over rice mixture. Bake uncovered 25-30 minutes, or until top is golden brown.

Turkey Hash Browns with Dijon Gravy

Yield: 4 servings

Gravy:
- 2 tablespoons butter
- 3 tablespoons flour
- 1 cup chicken broth
- 1/4 cup beef broth
- 1 teaspoon Kitchen Bouquet
- 2 tablespoons prepared Dijon mustard

Hash browns:
- 3 large baked potatoes, cooled, peeled and coarsely grated
- 1 1/2 cups coarsely shredded, cooked turkey
- 1 medium onion, chopped
- 1/2 cup (1 stick) butter
- 1 bunch (6-8) scallions, chopped, for garnish

In a small saucepan, melt butter over medium heat. Add flour and cook 3 minutes, stirring constantly. Add chicken broth, beef broth, Kitchen Bouquet and mustard; whisk until well blended. Cook until thick, stirring often.

In a large bowl, mix together potatoes, turkey and onions.

Melt butter in a 10-inch skillet over medium-high heat. Add potato mixture and cook until bottom is browned, approximately 10 minutes. Flip hash browns and cook other side for an additional 5 minutes. Remove from heat. Divide into 4 servings and garnish with scallions. Serve warm Dijon Gravy on the side.

Door County Omelet Filling

Yield: filling for 4 omelets

1   cup diced onions
1   cup diced peppers
2   cups sliced mushrooms
1   tablespoon butter
1/2   pound chopped ham
2   cups shredded Cheddar cheese, divided
    Sour cream, for garnish
    Parsley, for garnish

In a medium saucepan, sauté onions, peppers and mushrooms in butter until tender. Add ham and heat through.

Prepare a 2-egg omelet in a small Teflon-coated skillet. Add one quarter of the ham and vegetable mixture and 1/4 cup of the shredded cheese. Fold omelet in half. Top with 1/4 cup of the shredded cheese, cooking until eggs are set and cheese melts. Remove from pan and garnish with sour cream and parsley. Continue process until all omelets have been prepared. Serve immediately.

Omelet Olé Filling

Yield: filling for 4 omelets

1/4	cup olive oil
1	onion, finely chopped
3/4	cup chopped green pepper
1	tablespoon chopped garlic
1	can (15 ounces) black beans, drained
1 1/2	cups tomatoes, seeded and chopped
1	tablespoon cumin
1	tablespoon oregano
1/4	teaspoon cayenne pepper
1	tablespoon paprika
1	can (4 ounces) green chilies, diced and drained
1/2	teaspoon salt
1	cup shredded Cheddar cheese, divided
1	cup salsa (room temperature), divided
	Sour cream, for garnish

Heat oil in a medium saucepan. Sauté onion, green pepper and garlic until tender. Add beans, tomatoes, cumin, oregano, cayenne pepper, paprika, chilies and salt. Simmer 15 minutes.

Prepare a 2-egg omelet in a small Teflon-coated skillet. Add one-quarter of the filling and fold omelet in half. Top with 1/4 cup cheese and 1/4 cup salsa. Place cover over skillet and cook eggs until set and cheese melts. Remove from pan and garnish with sour cream. Continue process until all omelets have been prepared. Serve immediately.

Buttermilk Biscuits with Sausage Gravy

Yield: 6 servings

Biscuits:
- 2 1/4 cups flour
- 1 tablespoon plus 1 teaspoon baking powder
- 1/2 teaspoon salt
- 1/3 cup butter
- 3/4 cup buttermilk

Gravy:
- 18 cooked sausage links
- 3 tablespoons butter or margarine
- 1 medium onion, chopped
- 4 tablespoons flour
- 4 cups milk
- 1/2 cup heavy whipping cream
- 1 tablespoon dried, crushed thyme leaves
- 1 1/2 teaspoons pepper

Preheat oven to 425 degrees.

In a large bowl, combine flour, baking powder and salt. Cut in butter until mixture resembles coarse crumbs. Add buttermilk and knead just until well mixed. Place dough on a floured surface and roll to a thickness of 1 inch. Cut into 6 biscuits using a 3-inch round cutter. Place on ungreased cookie sheet and bake 12-15 minutes, or until golden brown. Remove from oven; cool slightly.

Using a meat grinder, grind half of the sausage and coarsely chop remaining half; set aside.

Melt butter in a medium saucepan. Add onions and cook until translucent. Add flour and cook over medium heat 1 minute, stirring constantly. Add milk, whipping cream, thyme and pepper; cook until thick, stirring often. Add sausage and heat through. To serve, cut biscuits in half and top with warm Sausage Gravy.

French Canadian Quiche

Yield: 12 servings

11/2 sheets (9 x 9 inches each) puff pastry
12   eggs
2   cups heavy whipping cream
1   teaspoon salt
1   teaspoon nutmeg
1/2 teaspoon white pepper
1   pound Canadian bacon, diced
1/2 pound Brie cheese, cut into 1/4-inch slices

Preheat oven to 325 degrees. Generously spray a 9-inch deep-dish quiche pan with nonstick cooking spray. Make one large sheet of puff pastry by over-lapping one edge of both sheets by 11/2 inches. Press edges together to seal. Place puff pastry in bottom and up sides of quiche pan, patching as necessary.

In a large mixing bowl, combine eggs, whipping cream, salt, nutmeg and white pepper with electric mixer on medium speed until well blended; set aside.

Sprinkle bacon evenly in bottom of pastry-lined pan and top with cheese slices. Pour egg mixture over all. Place pan on baking sheet and bake 1 hour, or until top of quiche is firm to the touch. Remove from oven and serve immediately.

Note: Quiche may be made in an 8-inch unbaked pie shell by dividing recipe in half. Yield: 6 servings.

Crab, Artichoke Heart and Cream Cheese Quiche

Yield: 12 servings

11/2 sheets (9 x 9 inches each) puff pastry
   12 eggs
    2 cups heavy whipping cream
    1 teaspoon salt
    1 teaspoon nutmeg
  1/2 teaspoon white pepper
    1 package (8 ounces) cream cheese
  6-8 ounces crabmeat
    1 can (14-ounces) artichoke hearts,
         drained and quartered

Preheat oven to 325 degrees. Generously spray a 9-inch deep-dish quiche pan with nonstick cooking spray. Make one large sheet of puff pastry by over-lapping one edge of both sheets by 11/2 inches. Press edges together to seal. Place puff pastry in bottom and up sides of quiche pan, patching as necessary.

In a large mixing bowl, combine eggs, whipping cream, salt, nutmeg and white pepper with electric mixer on medium speed until well blended; set aside.

Cut cream cheese in small cubes. Place crabmeat, cream cheese cubes and artichoke hearts evenly in prepared pan. Pour egg mixture over top. Place quiche pan on baking sheet and bake 1 hour, or until top of quiche is firm to the touch. Remove from oven and serve immediately.

Note: Quiche may be made in an 8-inch unbaked pie shell by dividing recipe in half. Yield: 6 servings.

BREADS

Morning Cinnamon Rolls

Photo on page 72

Yield: 9 large rolls

Dough:
- 1/4 pound (1 stick) butter
- 1 cup milk
- 1/2 cup granulated sugar
- 1 1/2 teaspoons salt
- 4-4 1/2 cups flour, divided
- 2 tablespoons rapid rise yeast
- 2 eggs, lightly beaten

Filling:
- 1 cup brown sugar
- 1 teaspoon cinnamon
- 4 tablespoons butter, melted

Frosting:
- 5 tablespoons butter, softened
- 2 cups powdered sugar
- 1/4 cup milk
- 1 teaspoon vanilla extract

In a medium saucepan, heat butter, milk, granulated sugar and salt to 120-130 degrees. Remove from heat.

In a large bowl, stir together 3 cups of the flour and yeast. Add milk mixture and eggs to flour; mix until smooth. Gradually add remaining 1 1/2 cups flour until dough is firm and not sticky to the touch. Turn dough onto a lightly floured surface and knead for about 5 minutes, or until smooth and elastic. Place in a greased bowl. Spray top of dough with cooking spray and cover loosely with plastic wrap. Place in a warm, draft-free area and allow to double in size, approximately 1 hour.

While dough is rising, stir brown sugar and cinnamon together in a small bowl; set aside.

Punch down dough. On a lightly floured surface, roll dough into an 18 x 14-inch rectangle. Brush with melted butter and sprinkle evenly with brown sugar/cinnamon mixture. Roll dough tightly, beginning with the 18-inch side. Pinch edge of dough to seal. Cut dough into nine, 2-inch thick slices. Place slices on a well-greased cookie sheet and spray tops with cooking spray. Loosely cover with plastic wrap to keep dough from drying out. Return

(continued on page 33)

cookie sheet to draft-free area and allow rolls to double in size, approximately 30-45 minutes. Bake in a preheated 325-degree oven 15-20 minutes, or until golden brown. Remove from oven and allow to cool before frosting.

To make frosting, cream butter and powdered sugar together in a medium bowl or food processor. Add milk and mix until smooth. Stir in vanilla. Spread over tops of cooled rolls.

Banana Walnut Muffins

Yield: 12 muffins

1/4   cup (1/2 stick) butter, softened
1/2   cup sugar
  2   eggs
  2   tablespoons milk
  2   medium ripe bananas
  2   cups flour
11/2   teaspoons baking powder
  1   teaspoon baking soda
     Pinch of salt
1/2   cup chopped walnuts

Preheat oven to 350 degrees. Spray a 12-cup muffin pan with nonstick cooking spray.

Using an electric mixer on high, cream butter and sugar together in a large bowl. Add eggs, milk and bananas; mix well.

In a separate bowl, combine flour, baking powder, baking soda and salt. Stir dry ingredients into creamed mixture just until moistened. Add nuts. Spoon batter into muffin cups, filling each cup three-quarters full. Bake 20 minutes, or until muffin springs back when lightly touched.

Bran Muffins with Cream Cheese Filling

Yield: 12 muffins

Muffins:
- 1 1/4 cups bran cereal
- 1 cup milk
- 1/4 cup oil
- 1 egg
- 1 1/4 cups flour
- 1/2 cup sugar
- 1 tablespoon baking powder
- 1/2 teaspoon salt
- 1/2 cup raisins

Filling:
- 4 ounces cream cheese, softened
- 2 tablespoons sugar
- 1 egg

Preheat oven to 375 degrees. Spray a 12-cup muffin pan with nonstick cooking spray and lightly dust with flour.

In a medium bowl, combine cereal and milk; let stand 2 minutes. Add oil and egg; mix well.

In a separate bowl, combine flour, sugar, baking powder and salt. Add to cereal mixture and stir until just moistened. Fold in raisins. Spoon batter into muffin cups, filling each cup two-thirds full.

To make filling, combine cream cheese, sugar and egg in a small bowl; mix until well blended. Spoon 1 rounded tablespoon on top of each muffin. Bake 25 minutes, or until muffin springs back when lightly touched.

Maple Pecan Scones with Maple Butter

Yield: 12 scones

3 cups flour
1 cup chopped pecans
1 1/2 tablespoons baking powder
1/2 teaspoon salt
3/4 cup butter, chilled
2/3 cup Door County maple syrup,
    plus additional syrup
    for brushing scones
1/3 cup heavy whipping cream

Maple Butter:
3/4 cup Door County maple syrup
9 tablespoons butter, softened

Preheat oven to 350 degrees. Spray a baking sheet with nonstick cooking spray and lightly dust with flour; set aside.

Using a fork, stir together flour, pecans, baking powder and salt in a large bowl. Cut in butter with a pastry blender until mixture resembles coarse meal. In a medium bowl, whisk together maple syrup and cream. Make a well in center of dry ingredients. Slowly pour in cream mixture, combining with swift strokes just until dough sticks together. (Dough will be firm.)

On a lightly floured surface, roll dough to a thickness of 2 inches (scones will not rise much higher than this when baked). Cut scones with a round biscuit cutter and place on prepared baking sheet about 2 inches apart. Brush tops with additional maple syrup. Bake 15-20 minutes, or until tops are lightly browned.

To make Maple Butter, cook maple syrup over low heat in a heavy saucepan without stirring, until it reaches the soft ball stage (234 degrees on a candy thermometer). Stir in butter. Pour mixture into a deep bowl and beat with electric mixer until thick and creamy, about 4 minutes. Serve with warm scones.

Candlelight Dinner Tied Rolls

Yield: 12 rolls

1/2 cup milk
1/4 cup sugar
3/4 teaspoon salt
1/4 cup (1/2 stick) butter, melted
2 packages (1/4 ounce each) active dry yeast
1/4 cup warm water (105-115 degrees F)
1 egg
21/2 cups flour, divided

Glaze:
1 egg white
1 tablespoon water

In a small saucepan, scald milk, sugar and salt. Cool slightly and stir in butter.

In a large bowl, dissolve yeast in 1/4 cup warm water. Stir in egg. Add 11/4 cups of the flour and mix well. Add scalded milk and remaining 11/4 cups flour alternately to yeast mixture, ending with flour. Turn onto a floured surface and knead 4-5 minutes, or until dough is elastic. Place in a greased bowl, turning dough so that it is greased on all sides. Cover with a damp cloth and set in a warm, draft-free place until dough has doubled in size, approximately 1 hour.

When dough has finished rising, punch down. Divide into 12 uniform pieces. Roll each piece on table top or between your hands to form a 12-inch long rope. Tie into a knot, tucking loose ends underneath. Place rolls on a greased cookie sheet. Return to a warm spot and allow dough to rise until doubled, approximately 45 minutes.

Heat oven to 375 degrees. Using a fork, beat egg white and water in a small bowl. Gently brush tops of rolls and bake 12-18 minutes, or until golden brown.

Lemon Bread

Yield: 1 loaf

1 1/4	cups sugar	2	cups flour
1/2	cup vegetable oil	1/2	teaspoon salt
4	teaspoons grated lemon rind	3 1/2	teaspoons baking powder
2	teaspoons lemon extract	3/4	cup milk
2	eggs		

Preheat oven to 350 degrees. Spray a 9 x 5-inch loaf pan with nonstick cooking spray. In a large bowl, beat together sugar, oil, lemon rind and lemon extract. Add eggs and continue beating until well combined, about 2-3 minutes.

In a separate bowl, sift together flour, salt, and baking powder. Alternately add dry ingredients and milk to creamed mixture. Pour into prepared pan and bake 60-65 minutes, or until a knife inserted in center of loaf comes out clean. Remove from oven and cool 10 minutes in pan. Remove loaf from pan and cool completely on wire rack.

Blueberry Bread

Yield: 1 loaf

1 1/4	cups sugar	1/2	teaspoon salt
1/2	cup vegetable oil	1/2	teaspoon baking powder
2	eggs	2/3	cup milk
1 3/4	cups flour	1	cup blueberries

Preheat oven to 350 degrees. Spray a 9 x 5-inch loaf pan with nonstick cooking spray. In a large bowl, beat together sugar and oil until well combined. Add eggs and continue beating, 2-3 minutes more.

In a separate bowl, sift together flour, salt and baking powder. Alternately add dry ingredients and milk to creamed mixture; beat until smooth. Gently fold in blueberries. Pour batter into prepared pan and bake 60-65 minutes, or until a knife inserted in center comes out clean. Cool 10 minutes in pan. Remove loaf from pan and cool completely on wire rack.

Steve's Swedish Limpa Bread

Yield: 3 loaves

Rind of 1 orange, grated	1 3/4 cups water, divided
1 1/2 cups buttermilk	2 packages (1/4-ounce each)
1 cup brown sugar, firmly packed	dry yeast
1/4 cup molasses	2 eggs, slightly beaten
1 1/2 tablespoons caraway seed	8-9 cups sifted unbleached flour,
1 1/2 teaspoons salt	divided
1 1/2 teaspoons anise seed	2 cups rye flour

In a medium saucepan, heat orange rind, buttermilk, brown sugar, molasses, caraway seed, salt, anise seed and 1 cup of the water over medium heat until mixture is warm and brown sugar is dissolved; set aside.

Heat remaining 3/4 cup water to 110-115 degrees. In a small mixing bowl, combine yeast, warm water and eggs. Mix thoroughly and let stand until yeast is fully dissolved.

In a large mixing bowl, combine 3 cups of the unbleached flour and the yeast mixture. Add half of the buttermilk mixture and stir well. Add rye flour and stir to combine. Add remaining buttermilk mixture and stir to blend. Add remaining 5 cups unbleached flour, one cup at a time, until dough is no longer sticky. Knead dough on a lightly floured surface for approximately 5 minutes, or until dough is smooth and no lumps remain. Place dough in a greased bowl, turning once to grease entire surface. Cover bowl with a clean towel or plastic wrap and set in a warm, draft-free spot. Allow to rise until doubled in size, approximately 1 hour. Punch down dough and divide into 3 equal parts. Shape into loaves.

Spray three 9 x 5-inch loaf pans with nonstick cooking spray. Place loaves in prepared pans. Return to a draft-free spot and let rise until doubled in size, approximately 1 hour. Bake in a preheated, 375-degree oven for 30-35 minutes. Remove bread from pans and cool on wire rack before slicing.

SOUPS

Hearty Beef Barley Soup

Yield: 10-12 servings

4 tablespoons (1/2 stick) butter
2 teaspoons minced garlic
1 cup chopped onions
1 cup chopped celery
1 cup diced red peppers
1 cup diced carrots
2 cups cubed beef
1 tablespoon dried thyme
2 teaspoons onion powder
1 teaspoon white pepper
2 bay leaves
4 quarts beef stock
13/4 cups barley

In a large stockpot, melt butter over medium-high heat. Add garlic, onions, celery, peppers, carrots and beef. Sauté until onions are tender. Add thyme, onion powder, white pepper, bay leaves and beef stock. Bring to a boil. Reduce heat and simmer for 1-11/2 hours. Stir in barley and continue to simmer 30 minutes or until barley is tender.

Cream of Garlic and Onion Soup

Yield: 6 servings

2 tablespoons butter
1 large white onion, finely diced
2 tablespoons minced garlic
1 large can (49 1/2 ounces) chicken broth
1/2 cup heavy whipping cream
1 1/2 teaspoons dried thyme leaves
1 teaspoon white pepper
2 tablespoons butter, melted
2 tablespoons flour
Chopped fresh parsley or chives, for garnish

Melt butter in a medium saucepan; add onion and garlic. Sauté over medium heat until tender but not brown, approximately 5 minutes. Add chicken broth, whipping cream, thyme and white pepper. Stir to blend and cook over medium heat 20 minutes more.

Stir together melted butter and flour in a small bowl. Whisk mixture into simmering soup until soup begins to thicken. Simmer an additional 15 minutes; remove from heat and cool slightly. Puree small batches of soup in blender. Return soup to saucepan and heat through. To serve, garnish with parsley or chives.

Cream of Mushroom with Wild Rice Soup

Yield: 6-8 servings

1/2 cup (1 stick) butter
1 medium onion, chopped
1 cup flour
6 cups chicken broth
4 cups sliced mushrooms
1 teaspoon dried thyme leaves
1 teaspoon pepper
2 cups cooked wild rice
1 cup heavy whipping cream

Melt butter in a medium saucepan. Add onions and cook over medium heat until tender. Add flour and cook, stirring constantly to create a roux, about 3 minutes. Whisk in chicken broth and mix until roux and broth are well blended. Stir in mushrooms and continue to heat until boiling. Reduce heat to low; add thyme, pepper and wild rice. Simmer until mushrooms are tender. Add cream and heat through.

Burgundy Mushroom Soup

Yield: 6 servings

      5 cups sliced mushrooms
      1 tablespoon butter
      1 tablespoon dried thyme leaves
      1 teaspoon pepper
  2 1/2 cups burgundy wine
      6 cups beef broth
      4 tablespoons cornstarch
    1/2 cup cold water

In a medium stockpot, sauté mushrooms in butter until tender. Add thyme, pepper and wine. Bring to a boil. Add beef broth; return to a boil. Reduce heat and simmer 30 minutes.

Mix cornstarch and cold water. Slowly add to soup, stirring constantly. Bring soup to a boil and boil 1 minute; reduce heat. Continue to simmer, stirring occasionally, until thick.

Red Bell Pepper Bisque

Yield: 8-10 servings

1/4 cup (1/2 stick) butter
1 cup chopped onions
2 teaspoons minced garlic
5 medium red bell peppers, diced
1 tablespoon dried thyme leaves
1/2-1 teaspoon crushed red pepper
1 large can (491/2 ounces) chicken stock
3/4 cup heavy whipping cream
1/2 cup uncooked white rice
Chopped parsley, for garnish

Melt butter in a large saucepan. Add onions, garlic and peppers; sauté over medium heat until vegetables are tender, approximately 5 minutes. Add thyme, crushed red pepper to taste, chicken stock, whipping cream and rice. Bring to a boil; reduce heat and simmer 30 minutes; cool slightly.

Process soup in small batches in a food processor or blender, until mixture becomes a fine puree. Return soup to saucepan and cook over low heat until heated through. Garnish with parsley.

Cream of Winter Squash Soup

Yield: 6-8 servings

2 tablespoons butter
2 carrots, peeled and coarsely chopped
1 onion, diced
3 leeks (white portion), coarsely chopped
2 medium butternut squash, peeled,
   seeded and coarsely chopped
6 cups chicken broth
1 cup heavy whipping cream
  Salt and pepper
  Cinnamon Croutons, for garnish

Melt butter in a medium saucepan. Add carrots, onion, leeks and squash; sauté for 5 minutes. Stir in chicken broth and bring to a boil. Reduce heat and simmer 30 minutes. Remove from heat and cool slightly.

Puree mixture in a blender or food processor in small batches. Return to saucepan. Add whipping cream, salt and pepper to taste. Heat through before serving. Garnish with Cinnamon Croutons (page 53), if desired.

Black Bean Soup

Yield: 8 servings

2 stalks celery, diced
1 medium onion, diced
1 green pepper, diced
1 red pepper, diced
2 tablespoons minced garlic
2 tablespoons olive oil
2 tablespoons ground cumin
1 1/2 tablespoons chili powder
1 tablespoon dried thyme leaves
4 cans (15 ounces each) black beans, undrained
1 jar (16 ounces) mild or medium salsa
Sour cream, for garnish
Shredded Cheddar cheese, for garnish

In a large stock pot over medium heat, sauté celery, onion, peppers and garlic in olive oil until tender, approximately 5-7 minutes. Add cumin, chili powder and thyme. Cook 2 or 3 minutes more. Stir in black beans and salsa and simmer for 30 minutes. Serve topped with sour cream and shredded Cheddar cheese.

Tomato Dill Soup

Yield: 8–10 servings

7	tablespoons butter, divided
5	tablespoons flour
1	cup diced onions
1/2	teaspoon chopped garlic
4	cups chicken broth
1	can (29 ounces) tomato sauce
1	can (28 ounces) diced tomatoes
2-3	dashes Tabasco sauce
1/4	cup honey
11/2	tablespoons dried dill weed
1/2	teaspoon black pepper
1/2	teaspoon chili powder
1/2	teaspoon dried basil
1/2	teaspoon dried thyme leaves
1/2	teaspoon lemon juice

In a small saucepan, melt 5 tablespoons of the butter. Quickly stir in flour and cook over medium heat 3-5 minutes, stirring constantly. Remove from heat and set aside.

In a large, heavy stockpot, melt remaining 2 tablespoons butter over medium-high heat. Add onions and garlic; sauté until onions are tender and translucent. Add chicken broth and bring to a boil. Reduce heat to simmer and whisk in butter and flour mixture. Cook over medium heat, stirring until soup becomes thick and smooth. Add tomato sauce, tomatoes, Tabasco, honey, dill weed, pepper, chili powder, basil, thyme and lemon juice; bring to a boil. Reduce heat and simmer 30 minutes, stirring often.

Italian Vegetable Soup

Yield: 6-8 servings

1/4 cup (1/2 stick) butter
1 cup sliced mushrooms
1 cup chopped celery
1 cup chopped carrots
1 cup sliced zucchini
1 cup chopped broccoli
1 cup chopped cauliflower
1 cup shredded cabbage
1/2 cup chopped green pepper
1/2 cup chopped red pepper
1/2 cup chopped onion
1 tablespoon chopped garlic
1 tablespoon dried basil
1 tablespoon dried oregano
1 tablespoon dried thyme leaves
2 teaspoons salt
11/2 teaspoons pepper
1 can (46 ounces) tomato juice
1/4 cup honey
2 cups water
1 can (6 ounces) tomato paste
Freshly grated Romano cheese, for garnish

Melt butter in a large stockpot. Add mushrooms, celery, carrots, zucchini, broccoli, cauliflower, cabbage, peppers, onion, garlic, basil, oregano, thyme, salt and pepper. Cook over medium heat, stirring occasionally, until vegetables are tender, about 5-10 minutes. Add tomato juice, honey, water and tomato paste. Bring to a boil. Reduce heat and simmer 30 minutes. Garnish with Romano cheese before serving.

Award Winning 3-Bean Chicken Chili

Yield: 8 servings

1   cup diced yellow onions
2   stalks celery, diced
1   tablespoon vegetable oil
4   cups diced chicken
2   cans (4 ounces each) diced green chilies
1   can (15 ounces) red kidney beans, undrained
1   can (15 ounces) garbanzo beans, undrained
1   can (15 ounces) navy beans, undrained
1   tablespoon dried thyme leaves
3   tablespoons chili powder
2   tablespoons cumin
1   tablespoon Mrs. Dash's seasoning blend
3   cups chicken broth
1   teaspoon salt

In a large stockpot, sauté onions and celery in vegetable oil over medium-high heat. Add chicken and cook 3-4 minutes. Add chilies, kidney beans, garbanzo beans, navy beans, thyme, chili powder, cumin, Mrs. Dash's, chicken broth and salt. Bring to a boil; reduce heat and simmer 30 minutes.

Chicken Almond Soup

Yield: 6 servings

1/2 cup (1 stick) butter
  1 cup chopped onion
  1 cup chopped celery
1/2 cup flour
  4 cups chicken stock
  2 cups cooked, boned and diced chicken
     Dash of white pepper
  1 tablespoon plus 1 teaspoon almond extract
1/2 cup heavy whipping cream
     Slivered almonds, for garnish

Melt butter in a large saucepan. Add onion and celery. Cook over medium heat until onions are transparent, approximately 4 minutes. Reduce heat. Add flour all at once and cook 3 minutes, stirring constantly. Whisk in chicken stock and stir until smooth. Add chicken, white pepper to taste, almond extract and whipping cream. Return to boil. Reduce heat to simmer. Cook an additional 15 minutes, stirring frequently. Garnish with slivered almonds.

Wisconsin Beer Cheese Soup

Yield: 8–10 servings

1	cup (2 sticks) butter
11/2	cups chopped onion
11/2	cups chopped celery
11/2	cups flour
6	cups chicken broth
21/2	cups chopped carrot
11/2	cups chopped green pepper
4	cups grated Wisconsin Cheddar cheese
1	bottle (12 ounces) Wisconsin beer
2	cups heavy whipping cream
	Salt and pepper

Melt butter in a 4-quart stock pot; add onion and celery and sauté until tender. Stir in flour all at once and cook over medium heat for 3 minutes, stirring constantly. Add chicken broth, carrots and green peppers. Stir briskly and continue to cook until thick. Reduce heat; add cheese. When cheese is melted, add beer and whipping cream. Cook over low heat, stirring often, until vegetables are tender, approximately 30 minutes. Season with salt and pepper to taste.

Door County Chilled Cherry Soup with Cinnamon Croutons

Yield: 4 servings

4 cups pitted Door County Montmorency
     or other tart cherries in unsweetened juice, divided
3 cups water
3/4 cup sugar
     Pinch of cinnamon
1/4 cup Kirsch
1/2 cup soda water
1/2 teaspoon almond extract
     Sour cream

In a medium saucepan, bring 2 cups of the cherries and juice, water, sugar and cinnamon to a boil. Reduce heat and simmer 10 minutes. Remove cherries and discard. Allow liquid to cool. Add Kirsch, soda water, almond extract and remaining 2 cups cherries and juice. Mix thoroughly and refrigerate. Serve chilled with a dollop of sour cream and Cinnamon Croutons (page 53).

Cinnamon Croutons

Yield: garnish for 4 servings of soup

2 slices dry white bread, cubed
1 tablespoon butter, melted
1 teaspoon cinnamon

Preheat oven to 375 degrees.

In a small bowl, toss bread cubes with melted butter and cinnamon until well coated. Place cubes on a cookie sheet and bake until golden brown, turning occasionally, about 10-15 minutes. Remove from oven and cool. Store in an airtight container.

Gazpacho Soup

Yield: 8 servings

6   tomatoes, chopped and seeded
1   cucumber, peeled, seeded and chopped
1   green bell pepper, seeded and chopped
2   jalapeno peppers, seeded and finely chopped
1   tablespoon lemon juice
2   teaspoons lime juice
1   medium yellow onion, finely chopped
2   cans (4 ounces each) chopped green chilies, drained
6   cups tomato juice
1   teaspoon salt
1/4   cup olive oil
2   teaspoons chopped garlic
1   tablespoon white vinegar
1/4   cup chopped parsley
1   tablespoon sugar
3/4   teaspoon Tabasco sauce, or to taste
1   teaspoon crushed red pepper, or to taste

Combine tomatoes, cucumber, green pepper, jalapeno peppers, lemon juice, lime juice, onion, chilies, tomato juice, salt, olive oil, garlic, vinegar, parsley, sugar, Tabasco and crushed red pepper in a large mixing bowl and stir until well blended. Add additional Tabasco and crushed red pepper to taste. Refrigerate; serve chilled.

DRESSINGS

Honey Lime Dressing

Yield: 1 1/2 cups

1/4 cup sugar
1/4 cup honey
1 tablespoon dry mustard
1 1/2 teaspoons ground ginger
3 1/2 tablespoons fresh lime juice
3 1/2 tablespoons water
3/4 cup olive or vegetable oil

Combine sugar, honey, mustard, ginger, lime juice and water in a blender. Blend for 30 seconds. Slowly add oil in a steady stream. Continue to blend until well combined.

Raspberry Vinaigrette Dressing

Yield: 3 1/2 cups

1 cup salad oil
1/2 cup olive oil
3/4 cup white vinegar
3/4 cup honey
2 cups whole raspberries
1 teaspoon freshly ground pepper
1/4 teaspoon salt

In large bowl of electric mixer, combine salad oil, olive oil, vinegar, honey, raspberries, pepper and salt. Stir together on low speed until well blended, approximately 2-3 minutes. (Do not whip at high speed.)

French Dressing

Yield: 1 1/2 cups

1/4	cup salad oil
1/2	cup ketchup
1	teaspoon lemon juice
1 1/2	teaspoons Worcestershire sauce
2	tablespoons white vinegar
3	tablespoons honey
2	tablespoons grated onion
1/4	cup sugar
1/2	teaspoon paprika
Scant 1/2	teaspoon salt
Scant 1/2	teaspoon pepper
1/2	teaspoon celery salt
1/4	teaspoon garlic powder

Mix oil, ketchup, lemon juice, Worcestershire, vinegar, honey, onion, sugar, paprika, salt, pepper, celery salt and garlic powder in a blender or food processor. Mix thoroughly.

Roasted Pecan Roquefort Dressing

Yield: 3 cups

2 cups sour cream
3/4 cup buttermilk
1/2 pound crumbled Roquefort
 or Bleu cheese (approximately 2 cups)
3/4 cup pecan pieces, salted and roasted

Mix sour cream, buttermilk and Roquefort in blender or by hand until well blended. Stir in pecan pieces.

Refrigerate until serving.

Creamy Parmesan Cracked Peppercorn Dressing

Yield: 3 cups

13/4	cups sour cream
1/4	cup buttermilk
1	tablespoon cracked black peppercorns
1/4	cup white vinegar
3/4	teaspoon salt
1	teaspoon garlic powder
1	teaspoon onion powder
1/3	cup salad oil
2	tablespoons honey
1/4	cup grated Parmesan cheese

Combine sour cream, buttermilk, peppercorns, vinegar, salt, garlic powder, onion powder, oil, honey and Parmesan in bowl of electric mixer, blender or food processor; mix well for 1-2 minutes. Refrigerate until serving.

Maple Syrup
and Balsamic Vinegar Dressing

Yield: 1¼ cups

1	teaspoon dry mustard
1/2	teaspoon dried basil
3	tablespoons balsamic vinegar
3	tablespoons Door County maple syrup
1	tablespoon lemon juice
1 or 2	cloves garlic, minced
1	cup olive oil
1¼	teaspoons salt
1/2	teaspoon freshly ground black pepper

In a medium bowl, stir together mustard and basil. Whisk in vinegar, maple syrup, lemon juice and garlic. Gradually whisk in olive oil and continue whisking until oil is well incorporated. Season with salt and pepper.

SALADS & SIDE DISHES

Grilled Chicken Salad
with Honey Lime Dressing

Photo on page 73

Yield: 6 servings as a main course

  6 chicken breast halves, skinned and boned
  9 cups mixed salad greens
  6 cups assorted fresh fruit
11/2 cups Honey Lime Dressing
11/2 cups roasted pecan pieces

Grill chicken breasts over an outdoor grill until thoroughly cooked; set aside to cool.

Divide salad greens evenly among 6 plates. Cut cooled chicken into slices and arrange over greens. Top each salad with 1 cup fruit and 1/4 cup Honey Lime Dressing (page 56). Garnish with pecan pieces.

Crabmeat and Wild Rice Salad

Photo on page 73

Yield: 8-10 servings as a main course

    2 cups wild rice
    4 cups water
       Pinch of salt
    2 bunches green onions, chopped
    1 red bell pepper, diced
    1 cup green peas
    1 cup sliced water chestnuts
    1 pound crabmeat

Dressing:
  1 1/2 cups mayonnaise
   1/2 cup red wine vinegar
   1/4 cup Dijon mustard

      Salt and pepper
      Lettuce leaves
      Fresh fruit, for garnish

In a medium saucepan, bring wild rice, water and salt to a boil. Reduce heat and simmer 35-45 minutes, or until rice is tender and water is absorbed. Fluff with a fork and set aside to cool.

Combine onions, bell pepper, peas, water chestnuts and crabmeat in a large bowl. Add rice and toss.

To make dressing, whisk together mayonnaise, vinegar and mustard in a small bowl until well combined. Add to rice and vegetables. Season with salt and pepper to taste. To serve, arrange salad on lettuce leaves on individual plates. Garnish with fresh fruit, if desired.

Tortellini Pesto Salad

Yield: 12 side dish servings
6 main course servings

5   cups cheese-filled tortellini
1   bunch green onions, sliced
3   cups broccoli flowerets
1   red bell pepper, diced
2   carrots, thinly sliced
1   cup Kalamata or black olives,
      pitted and sliced

Pesto dressing:
1/2   cup fresh parsley
1/2   cup fresh basil
1   tablespoon chopped garlic
1/2   cup freshly grated Parmesan cheese
1/4   cup olive oil
1/2   cup salad dressing
1/2   cup mayonnaise
1/2   cup milk
1/2   teaspoon salt
1/2   teaspoon freshly ground black pepper

Toasted pine nuts, for garnish

Cook tortellini in salted, boiling water until al dente, approximately 20 minutes. Do not overcook. Drain well and set aside to cool.

In a large bowl, combine onions, broccoli, red pepper, carrots and olives.

To prepare dressing, mix parsley, basil, garlic and Parmesan in a blender. With blender running, slowly drizzle in a steady stream of oil and blend until well combined. Transfer mixture to a medium bowl. Add salad dressing, mayonnaise, milk, salt and pepper; whisk together. Add cooled tortellini to vegetables; toss with pesto dressing, gently stirring to coat. Refrigerate until serving. Garnish with toasted pine nuts, if desired.

Curried Chicken Rice Salad

Yield: 6-8 servings

1 1/2	cups white rice
1	teaspoon salt
3 3/4	cups water
1 1/2	cups cooked chicken, cut into bite-size pieces
1	cup frozen peas, thawed
1/2	cup diced celery
1/4	cup green onions, thinly sliced
1/4	cup chopped fresh parsley
3/4	cup diced green pepper
3/4	cup raisins
1 1/2	cups mayonnaise
1/2	cup heavy whipping cream
3/4	tablespoon curry powder
	Lettuce leaves
1	cup sweetened, shredded coconut, toasted

Combine rice, salt and water in a 3-quart saucepan. Bring to a boil; stir once. Cover with a tight fitting lid and simmer over low heat for 20 minutes or until water is absorbed. Remove from heat and set aside to cool.

In a large bowl, mix together chicken, peas, celery, green onions, parsley, green pepper and raisins. Add cooled rice.

In a small bowl, whisk together mayonnaise, cream and curry powder. Add to rice and vegetable mixture, gently stirring to coat. Serve on a bed of lettuce leaves and top with toasted coconut.

Broccoli Salad

Yield: 4 servings as a side dish
2 servings as a main course

Dressing:

    1   cup mayonnaise
  1/4 cup sugar
  1/4 cup red wine vinegar
  1/2 teaspoon freshly ground black pepper

    6   slices bacon

Vegetables:

    4   cups broccoli flowerets,
       cut into small, bite-size pieces
  1/2 cup chopped onion
  1/2 cup sliced carrot
  1/3 cup diced red pepper

       Lettuce leaves
  1/2 cup shredded Cheddar cheese

Whisk together mayonnaise, sugar, vinegar and black pepper in a small bowl. Chill.

In a small skillet, fry bacon until crisp. Drain and cut into small pieces; set aside.

In a large bowl, toss together broccoli, onion, carrot and red pepper. Immediately before serving, pour dressing over vegetables and stir to coat. Arrange salad on a bed of lettuce leaves and top with shredded cheese and bacon.

Vegetable Barley Salad

Yield: 10-12 servings as a side dish

4 1/2 cups water
1 1/2 teaspoons salt
1 1/2 cups pearled barley
3 cups sliced mushrooms
1 1/2 cups shredded carrots
1/2 cup sliced green onions
1/2 cup diced red bell pepper

Dressing:
1/3 cup lemon juice
1 tablespoon chopped garlic
2 teaspoons prepared Dijon mustard
1 teaspoon dried tarragon
1/2 teaspoon freshly ground black pepper
3/4 cup vegetable oil
Salt and pepper

In a medium saucepan, bring water and salt to a boil. Stir in barley and simmer until water is absorbed and barley is tender, approximately 45 minutes. Rinse with cold water, drain well and chill.

In a large bowl, combine mushrooms, carrots, onions and pepper. Toss with chilled barley.

To make dressing, combine lemon juice, garlic, mustard, tarragon and black pepper in a small bowl. Whisk in oil in a slow, steady stream. Pour dressing over barley vegetable mixture and stir to coat. Add salt and pepper to taste. Serve chilled.

White Gull Inn Potato Salad

Yield: 12-14 servings

Dressing:

Pasteurized eggs equivalent to 3 medium eggs*
1/2 cup prepared Dijon mustard
1 tablespoon red wine vinegar
1 tablespoon fresh lemon juice
1 tablespoon dried dill
1 tablespoon salt
1/2 teaspoon pepper
1 tablespoon sugar
1/2 cup vegetable oil
1 1/4 cups sour cream

5 pounds small red potatoes, unpeeled
6 stalks celery, chopped
1 medium onion, chopped

In a blender, process eggs, mustard, vinegar, lemon juice, dill, salt, pepper and sugar on medium-high speed until slightly thickened. With machine running, gradually add oil in a steady stream and blend for 30 seconds more. Pour into a large bowl and stir in sour cream until well combined. Refrigerate.

Cook potatoes in salted water until just done. Do not overcook. Remove from heat and allow to cool. Cut potatoes into chunks and combine with celery and onions in a large bowl. Pour dressing over potatoes and stir until well coated. Chill 30 minutes and serve.

*Available at specialty food and larger grocery stores. Pasteurized eggs are recommended whenever eggs are not going to be cooked thoroughly.

White Gull Inn Coleslaw

Yield: 8 cups

6 cups grated green cabbage
1 cup grated carrots
1/4 cup chopped celery
1/4 cup grated radishes
2 tablespoons grated onion

Dressing:
1 cup Miracle Whip-type salad dressing
11/2 tablespoons white vinegar
2 tablespoons sugar
3/4 teaspoon celery salt
3/4 teaspoon caraway seed

In a large bowl, toss together cabbage, carrots, celery, radishes and onion.

In a separate small bowl, whisk together salad dressing, vinegar, sugar, celery salt and caraway seed. Refrigerate until serving. To serve, pour dressing over vegetables and stir to coat.

Winter Squash Casserole

Yield: 8-10 servings as a side dish

5 cups cooked, mashed acorn squash
  (approximately 2-3 squash)
7 tablespoons butter, divided
4 tablespoons brown sugar, divided
1/4 teaspoon salt
1/4 teaspoon pepper
4 cups unpeeled, sliced MacIntosh apples
  (approximately 3 apples)
1 tablespoon granulated sugar
2 cups Raisin Bran cereal, coarsely crushed
1/2 cup unsalted pecan halves

Preheat oven to 350 degrees. Spray 3-quart casserole dish with cooking spray. In a large bowl, mix squash, 4 tablespoons of the butter, 2 tablespoons of the brown sugar, salt and pepper; set aside.

In a medium saucepan, melt 1 tablespoon butter. Add apples and granulated sugar; cook gently for 3 minutes, or until apples are tender. Place cooked apples in the prepared casserole dish. Spread squash mixture over apples.

Mix cereal, 2 tablespoons of melted butter, remaining 2 tablespoons brown sugar and pecans in a medium bowl. Sprinkle over top of casserole. Bake 25-30 minutes until casserole is hot and topping is golden brown.

Montmorency Cherry Coffee Cake, *recipe on page 20*
Cherry Pancakes, *recipe on page 22*

clockwise from upper left:
Morning Cinnamon Roll, *recipe on page 32*
White Gull Inn Granola, *recipe on page 23*
Cherry and Cream Cheese Stuffed French Toast, *recipe on page 21*

clockwise from upper right:
Crabmeat and Wild Rice Salad, *recipe on page 63*
Open Doorwich with Honey Dijon Sauce, *recipe on page 78*
Grilled Chicken Salad with Honey Lime Dressing, *recipe on page 62*

Rosemary Baked Rack of Lamb, *recipe on page 104*

Raspberry Chicken Amandine, *recipe on page 100*

clockwise from upper right:
Door County Cherry Pie, *recipe on page 108*
Truffle Trio Torte, *recipe on page 124*
Macadamia Nut Tart with Grand Marnier Sauce, *recipe on page 128*
Apple Dumplings with Brandy Cream Sauce, *recipe on page 111*

SANDWICHES

Open Doorwich
with Honey Dijon Sauce

Photo on page 73

Yield: 4 servings

1-2 tablespoons butter
4 slices dark Bavarian rye bread
1 pound thinly sliced cooked ham
1 tart apple, cored and thinly sliced
6 ounces Brie cheese, sliced 1/4-inch thick
Paprika, for garnish

Butter one side of each slice of rye bread. Place bread, butter side down, in a large frying pan over medium heat. Place one-quarter of the ham on each bread slice. Top each sandwich with apple slices and Brie cheese. Cover pan and cook until cheese begins to melt. Remove pan from heat. Sprinkle sandwiches with paprika and serve with Honey Dijon Sauce on the side.

Honey Dijon Sauce

Yield: 2/3 cup

1/3 cup honey
1/3 cup Dijon mustard

Combine honey and mustard in a small bowl; mix well.

SANDWICHES

Pilgrim Sandwich

Yield: 4 sandwiches

8   slices dark rye bread
4   tablespoons mayonnaise
1   pound sliced or shaved cooked turkey breast
3/4   cup cranberry orange relish*
4   ounces Cheddar cheese, sliced
8   lettuce leaves

Place slices of rye bread on work surface. Spread mayonnaise on 4 of the slices. Top with turkey, relish, cheese and lettuce. Cover with remaining 4 slices rye bread and cut in half to serve.

*Available in most supermarkets.

SANDWICHES

Garden Sandwich
with Cucumber Dill Sauce

Yield: 4 servings

Butter
8 slices whole wheat bread
8 slices Swiss or Cheddar cheese (about 1/2 pound)
1 medium green pepper,
      seeded and sliced into thin rings
1 cup sliced mushrooms
1 cup alfalfa sprouts
8 tomato slices

Butter one side of each slice of bread. Set bread, butter side down, in a large frying pan over medium heat. Top each slice with one piece of cheese. Divide and layer vegetables over cheese and cook until cheese is melted and bread is golden brown. (Vegetables will remain uncooked and crisp.) Press bread slices together to form sandwiches. Serve with Cucumber Dill Sauce (page 81) on the side.

Cucumber Dill Sauce

Yield: 1 1/4 cups

1/4 cup chopped and seeded cucumber
1/4 teaspoon chopped garlic
1/2 cup mayonnaise
1/2 cup sour cream
1/2 teaspoon dried dill

To make sauce, combine cucumber, garlic, mayonnaise, sour cream and dried dill in a small bowl; mix thoroughly.

Vegetable Burgers

Yield: 8 patties

1/2 cup finely chopped cauliflower
1/2 cup finely chopped broccoli
1/2 cup finely chopped mushrooms
1/2 cup shredded carrots
1/4 cup finely chopped onion
1/4 cup finely chopped red bell pepper
1 tablespoon chopped garlic
1 teaspoon dried whole leaf thyme
1 1/2 cups textured vegetable protein*
1 1/2 cups egg substitute
1 tablespoon soy sauce
1/4 cup water chestnuts, finely chopped
1 1/2 teaspoons salt
3/4 teaspoon onion powder
1/2 teaspoon garlic powder
3/4 cup unseasoned bread crumbs

Begin recipe the day before serving. Combine cauliflower, broccoli, mushrooms, carrots, onion, bell pepper, garlic and thyme in a nonstick skillet. Sauté on medium-low heat until tender.

While vegetables are cooking, mix vegetable protein, egg substitute, soy sauce, water chestnuts, salt, onion powder, garlic powder and bread crumbs in a medium bowl. Stir cooked vegetables into vegetable protein mixture. Chill overnight.

Form mixture into eight, 4-ounce patties. Spray skillet with nonstick cooking spray and cook patties over medium heat, about 3-4 minutes on each side.

*Available in most health food stores.

APPETIZERS

Alaskan Crab Cakes

Yield: 6 cakes

4 tablespoons (1/2 stick) butter, divided
3 tablespoons minced white onion
1/2 cup minced celery
1 red bell pepper, diced
3/4 cup dried plain bread crumbs
2 eggs, slightly beaten
2 cups crabmeat, pre-cooked
1/2 teaspoon dry mustard
2 teaspoons chopped parsley
1 teaspoon dried thyme leaves
1 teaspoon dried tarragon leaves
1/2 teaspoon salt
1 teaspoon paprika

Preheat oven to 350 degrees.

Melt 2 tablespoons of the butter in a medium saucepan over medium-high heat. Sauté onion, celery and pepper until onion is transparent, approximately 3-4 minutes. Remove from heat. Add bread crumbs, eggs, crabmeat, mustard, parsley, thyme, tarragon, salt and paprika; mix well. Shape mixture into 6 patties or cakes.

In a large frying pan, melt remaining 2 tablespoons butter and sauté cakes until golden brown on each side. Transfer cakes to a baking sheet; bake 5 minutes. Serve immediately on a bed of warm Braised Black Beans (page 85). Top with Pineapple Salsa (page 85).

Pineapple Salsa

Yield: approximately 1 cup

1 cup crushed fresh pineapple, drained
1 tablespoon red wine vinegar
1 tablespoon diced red bell pepper
1 tablespoon diced green bell pepper
1 tablespoon diced red onion
1 tablespoon minced parsley
1 tablespoon minced cilantro
1 teaspoon cumin
Salt and pepper

Mix pineapple, vinegar, peppers, onion, parsley, cilantro and cumin in a small bowl. Add salt and pepper to taste. Let stand at least 2 hours. Chill before serving.

Braised Black Beans

Yield: approximately 2 cups

1 can (15 ounces) black beans, drained
1 teaspoon cumin
1 teaspoon dried thyme leaves
1/4 teaspoon crushed red pepper
1/2 teaspoon onion powder
1/2 teaspoon garlic powder
1/4 cup dry sherry
Salt and pepper

Place beans, cumin, thyme, crushed red pepper, onion powder, garlic powder and sherry in a small saucepan. Cover and simmer 15 minutes. Adjust seasoning with salt and pepper to taste.

Scallops in Puff Pastry with Roasted Red Bell Pepper Sauce

Yield: 6 appetizer servings
2-3 main course servings

      1   sheet (91/2 x 91/2-inches) frozen puff pastry
    2/3   cup grated Baby Swiss cheese
      2   ounces precooked shrimp, deveined and chopped
      2   ounces precooked crabmeat
      6   extra large or 12 large sea scallops, steamed

Preheat oven to 400 degrees.

Thaw pastry according to package instructions. Cut into 6 uniform-size pieces (roughly 43/4 x 3-inches). With rolling pin or fingers, work each piece of pastry into a perfect square. Divide Swiss cheese, shrimp and crabmeat evenly over squares. Top with scallops. Fold four corners of pastry square together, sealing seams well. Place seam side down on an ungreased baking sheet and bake 15-20 minutes, or until golden brown. Remove from oven. Place pastry on top of warm Roasted Red Bell Pepper Sauce (page 87) and serve immediately.

Roasted Red Bell Pepper Sauce

Yield: 2 1/2 cups

1	red bell pepper
1	tablespoon minced garlic
1	teaspoon dried thyme leaves
	Pinch of cayenne pepper
1/4	cup (1/2 stick) butter, softened
1/3	cup flour
1 1/2	cups chicken stock
1/2	cup heavy whipping cream

Over an open flame, turn whole red pepper until completely blackened. Place pepper in a paper sack for 5 minutes and allow to steam. Remove from sack and peel off charred skin. Remove stem and seeds and dice.

In a medium frying pan, sauté peppers, garlic, thyme and cayenne over medium heat.

In a separate bowl, stir together butter and flour to create a roux. Add to frying pan and cook 3-4 minutes, stirring constantly. Add chicken stock and whipping cream and stir until smooth. Simmer 5 minutes. Remove from heat and cool slightly. In batches, process in blender on high speed for 15 seconds. Return to pan and heat through.

Baked Brie and Fruit in Puff Pastry

Yield: 4-6 servings

1 sheet (9 1/2 x 9 1/2 inches) frozen puff pastry, thawed
1/2 cup slightly mashed fresh berries of your choice,
    or sliced fresh apricots
1/4 cup chopped walnuts
1 round (8 ounces) Brie cheese
1 loaf French bread

Preheat oven to 400 degrees.

Place a sheet of puff pastry on work surface. Pile fresh fruit and chopped nuts in center. Place round of Brie over fruit, and fold corners of pastry around Brie. Pinch seams together to seal. Trim any excess pastry if necessary. Place on baking sheet and bake 15-20 minutes, or until pastry is golden brown. Remove from oven and cool slightly. Serve immediately with French bread.

Buckwheat Scones with Smoked Salmon and Cream Cheese

Yield: 6 servings

Cream Cheese:
- 2 packages (3 ounces each) cream cheese, softened
- 2 teaspoons chopped capers
- 2 teaspoons lime juice
- 1 large shallot, minced
- 1/4 teaspoon white pepper

Scones:
- 11/3 cups all-purpose flour
- 2/3 cup buckwheat flour
- 1/2 teaspoon dried dill
- 1 teaspoon baking powder
- 1 teaspoon baking soda
- 1/4 teaspoon salt
- 4 tablespoons cold butter, cut into pieces
- 2/3 cup milk
- 6 ounces thinly sliced smoked salmon or lox
- Fresh dill or parsley, for garnish

In a medium bowl, mix together cream cheese, capers, lime juice, shallots and pepper until smooth. Roll mixture in plastic wrap to form a 6-inch log. Refrigerate at least 30 minutes.

Preheat oven to 400 degrees.

In a large bowl, combine all-purpose flour, buckwheat flour, dill, baking powder, baking soda and salt. With a pastry blender, cut in butter until mixture resembles fine crumbs. Stir in milk.

Turn dough onto a lightly floured surface and knead lightly ten times, adding flour if necessary. Roll or pat to a thickness of 1/2-inch. Cut into 6 circles with a floured 3-inch round cutter. Place on an ungreased baking sheet and bake until browned, 10-12 minutes. Immediately remove from baking sheet and allow to cool on wire rack.

To serve, split cooled scones in half. Slice cream cheese log into 12 even medallions. Place 2 medallions on one half of each scone. Divide smoked salmon and place on the other half of the scone. Garnish with a sprig of fresh dill or chopped parsley.

Herbed Spinach Cakes

Yield: 12 appetizer servings
6 main course servings

2 tablespoons butter	1/4 cup grated Parmesan or Romano cheese
1 1/2 cups chopped onions	1/2 teaspoon salt
4 tablespoons minced garlic	1/4 teaspoon pepper
2 teaspoons dried rosemary	2 eggs, slightly beaten
1/2 teaspoon dried nutmeg	3/4-1 cup dried bread crumbs
1 teaspoon dried thyme leaves	1 tablespoon vegetable oil
1 teaspoon dried parsley	1 1/2 cups shredded Mozzarella or Parmesan cheese
1 teaspoon dried basil	Italian marinara sauce (optional)
2 packages (10 ounces each) frozen chopped spinach, thawed and well drained	
2 1/2 cups mashed potatoes	

Preheat oven to 350 degrees.

In a large nonstick pan, melt butter over medium heat. Add onions and garlic; sauté 5 minutes. Add rosemary, nutmeg, thyme, parsley, basil and spinach. Cook 3-4 minutes, stirring occasionally. Place spinach mixture in a large bowl and cool 10 minutes. Add mashed potatoes, grated cheese, salt, pepper, eggs and enough bread crumbs to make mixture hold together; mix well. Form into 12 uniform-size patties.

In a large frying pan, sauté patties in vegetable oil over medium heat until golden brown, approximately 2 minutes per side. Place on a baking sheet and bake 5 minutes. Top with shredded Mozzarella or Parmesan cheese and return to oven until cheese begins to melt. Serve baked spinach cakes plain or on top of marinara sauce, if desired.

ENTREES

ENTREES

Macadamia Crusted Salmon with Lime Ginger Butter

Yield: 2 servings

1 egg
2 tablespoons milk
1 cup macadamia nuts
2 tablespoons yellow cornmeal
1 teaspoon salt
1/2 teaspoon white pepper
2 salmon fillets (about 6 ounces each)
2 tablespoons olive oil

Lime Ginger Butter:
4 tablespoons butter, at room temperature
1/8 teaspoon minced lime zest
1 teaspoon lime juice
Scant 1/2 teaspoon minced garlic
Scant 1/2 teaspoon honey
Scant 1/2 teaspoon minced fresh gingerroot
Pinch of salt
Pinch of pepper

Preheat oven to 350 degrees.

In a small bowl, whisk together egg and milk; set aside. Place macadamia nuts, cornmeal, salt and pepper in a food processor and pulse until fine. (Take care not to overprocess as nut oils will eventually form a paste.) Dip salmon fillets in egg wash and dredge in macadamia nuts, pressing nuts into fillets. Heat oil in a nonstick frying pan and sauté fillets over medium heat until lightly browned. Transfer to a baking pan and bake 25 minutes. Check for doneness.

In a small bowl, mix together butter, lime zest, lime juice, garlic, honey, gingerroot, salt and pepper until well combined. Place mixture on a sheet of waxed paper and roll into a log shape. Place in freezer while salmon finishes baking. To serve, slice into rounds and place over warm salmon.

ENTREES

Shrimp and Artichoke Romano

Yield: 2 servings

1/4 pound linguine
8 jumbo shrimp, deveined
6 artichoke hearts, cut in quarters lengthwise
2 tablespoons clarified butter
1 tablespoon minced garlic
Pinch of salt
Pinch of pepper
1/2 cup dry white wine
6 tablespoons grated Romano cheese
4 tablespoons unsalted butter, at room temperature
2 teaspoons freshly chopped parsley, for garnish

In boiling, salted water, cook linguine until al dente; set aside.

In a large frying pan, sauté shrimp and artichoke hearts in clarified butter for 2-3 minutes, or until shrimp is almost completely cooked through. Add garlic, salt and pepper and stir until garlic browns slightly, approximately 20 seconds. Add white wine and Romano cheese and simmer over medium heat until liquid is slightly thickened, approximately 30 seconds. Reduce heat and add unsalted butter, one tablespoon at a time, incorporating it into sauce using a swirling motion. Be careful not to let sauce boil. (Sauce will be the consistency of heavy cream.) Add cooked linguine and swirl pan to incorporate sauce; heat through. Garnish with chopped parsley and serve immediately.

Oriental Pan-Seared Sea Scallops

Yield: 2 servings

Marinade:
- 1/4 cup olive oil
- 2 tablespoons soy sauce
- 1 tablespoon sesame oil
- 1 tablespoon Chinese 5 spice powder
- 1/2 teaspoon crushed red pepper

- 12 sea scallops
- 1 tablespoon butter, melted
- 1 tablespoon sesame oil
- 1 cup sliced shiitake mushrooms

- 1 cup sliced green onions
- 1/2 cup sliced roasted red bell peppers*
- 10 ears baby corn
- 2 cups cooked linguine
- 2 tablespoons soy sauce
- 1/4-1/2 teaspoon crushed red pepper
- 1 tablespoon chopped parsley

To make marinade, in a small bowl, whisk together olive oil, soy sauce, sesame oil, spice powder and crushed red pepper. Place scallops in a shallow baking pan and pour marinade over all. Refrigerate at least two hours or overnight. Drain scallops and discard marinade.

In a large frying pan, heat butter and sesame oil over high heat until smoking. Add marinated scallops and cook untouched for 3 minutes. Turn scallops over and add mushrooms, onions, roasted red peppers and baby corn; sauté on high for about 4 minutes. Add cooked linguine and toss. Turn heat down to medium-high. Add soy sauce, crushed red pepper to taste and parsley; continue to sauté until liquid has evaporated from pan. Serve immediately.

*When roasting pepper, it is important that flames interact directly with the pepper to give this dish its smoky flavor. Roast pepper directly over flame until skin has turned completely black. Place pepper in a paper bag for 5 minutes to allow it to steam. Remove from bag and peel off charred skin. Remove seeds and stem. Do not rinse under water.

Wisconsin Walleye au Gratin

Yield: 8 servings

1 1/4	pounds fresh asparagus spears, cut into 1-inch pieces (about 5 cups)
3	pounds walleye pike fillets, skin and bones removed
12	tablespoons butter, divided
2	cups chopped onions
2/3	cup flour
3	cups milk
1/2	cup chicken broth
2 2/3	cups shredded Cheddar cheese
1/2	teaspoon salt
1/2	teaspoon pepper
2	cups crushed saltine crackers

Preheat oven to 350 degrees. Butter a 15 x 10-inch baking dish. Arrange asparagus evenly over bottom of pan. Place fillets on top of asparagus; set aside.

Melt 6 tablespoons of the butter in a 1-quart saucepan over low heat. Add onions and sauté until tender, about 3-5 minutes. Add flour and cook for 3 minutes, stirring constantly. Whisk in milk and chicken broth, stirring constantly. Cook until mixture thickens and begins to boil. Add cheese, salt and pepper. Remove from heat. Stir until cheese is melted. Pour warm cheese sauce evenly over walleye fillets.

In a 1-quart saucepan, melt remaining 6 tablespoons butter over low heat. Remove from heat. Add crushed saltines and stir until coated. Sprinkle crumb mixture evenly over cheese sauce. Bake fish covered for 30 minutes. Uncover pan and brown for 10-15 minutes, until sauce is hot and bubbly. Let stand 10 minutes before serving.

Note: Frozen asparagus may be substituted for fresh. Thaw and drain excess water before using.

Whitefish Oscar
with Hollandaise Sauce

Yield: 4 servings

16 asparagus spears
4 whitefish fillets (8-10 ounces each)
  Salt
  Pepper
8 ounces crabmeat, pre-cooked
  Lemon wedges, for garnish
  Fresh parsley, for garnish

Steam asparagus until just tender; set aside.

Turn oven to broil setting. Place fillets on a baking sheet and season with salt and pepper. Place baking sheet three or four inches from broiler. Broil on high until fish is firm, approximately 3-4 minutes. Remove pan from oven and top each fillet with 2 ounces of crabmeat and 4 spears of asparagus. Return baking sheet to broiler and broil until crab and asparagus are heated through, approximately 2-3 minutes.

Transfer broiled fish to serving dish and top each fillet with Hollandaise Sauce (page 97). Garnish with lemon wedges and parsley and serve immediately.

Hollandaise Sauce

Yield: 1 cup

1/2 cup Papetti's Pasteurized liquid egg yolks*
    (equivalent to six egg yolks)
2 tablespoons fresh lemon juice
8 tablespoons very hot melted butter

Whip egg yolks and lemon juice at high speed in blender until very smooth and bright yellow. Add butter slowly into blender while on high speed until mixture thickens. Serve immediately.

*Available at specialty food and larger grocery stores. Pasteurized eggs are recommended whenever eggs are not going to be cooked thoroughly.

ENTREES

White Gull Inn Fish Boil

Yield: 6 servings

Equipment:
  1 five-gallon pot
    Removable basket or net, or two 24 x 24-inch pieces
      of cheesecloth, or large colander

  8 quarts water
 12 small red potatoes
  2 cups salt, divided*
 12 whitefish steaks (with bones), about 2 inches thick
    Melted butter
    Lemon wedges, for garnish

At the White Gull Inn, we cook the fish outside over a wood fire, using a 22-gallon pot and two removable metal nets, one for the fish and one for the potatoes. This recipe has been adapted for the kitchen stove. You will need a large pot (5-gallon is ideal), preferably with a removable basket or net, for draining. For smaller quantities, as in this recipe, the fish and potatoes can be put in one basket or net. If your pot does not have a removable basket for draining, you can make a cheesecloth bag to hold the potatoes and another one to hold the fish. Or, gently transfer food to colander and allow to drain in sink.

Bring water to a boil in pot. Water should remain at a constant boil throughout cooking process.

Wash potatoes; cut a small slice off each end and discard ends. (This allows flavor from salt water to penetrate potato.) Add potatoes and 1 cup of the salt to boiling water; cook 20 minutes. Pierce potatoes with fork to check for doneness. (Potatoes should be slightly firm and fork should remove easily.) Add whitefish steaks and remaining 1 cup salt. Cook approximately 8-10 minutes, or until fish is still firm but begins to pull away from the bone when lifted with a fork. At the Inn, when cooking outside, we toss a small amount of kerosene on the fire when the fish is done, causing the fish oils, which have

(continued on page 99)

risen to the surface of the water, to boil over the sides. Do not attempt this at home; simply skim oil from surface with a spoon while fish is cooking.

Lift cooked potatoes and fish from water and drain. Serve immediately with melted butter and wedges of lemon.

Traditional fish boil accompaniments are White Gull Inn Coleslaw (page 69), homemade Steve's Swedish Limpa Bread (page 38), Lemon Bread (page 37) and Blueberry Bread (page 37), and Door County Cherry Pie (page 108) for dessert.

*The amount of salt used in the fish boil is based on the amount of water. To double the recipe, add 1 cup salt for each additional gallon of water.

Whitefish Parmesan

Yield: 4 servings

4   whitefish fillets (about 8-10 ounces each)
     Salt
     Pepper
1   cup freshly grated Parmesan cheese
     Chopped parsley, for garnish
     Lemon wedges, for garnish

Turn oven to broil setting. Place fillets on a baking sheet, skin side down. Season with salt and pepper to taste. Place baking sheet three to four inches from broiler and broil until fish is firm, about 3-4 minutes. Remove pan from oven and top each fillet with 1/4 cup Parmesan cheese. Return fillets to oven and continue broiling until Parmesan turns a golden brown, approximately 2-4 minutes. Sprinkle with chopped parsley. Serve immediately with a wedge of lemon.

Raspberry Chicken Amandine

Photo on page 75

Yield: 4 servings

Raspberry Sauce:
- 3 cups frozen raspberries
- 1 cup water
- 3/4 cup honey
- 2 tablespoons cornstarch
- 1/4 cup cold water
- Salt and pepper

Chicken:
- 2 eggs
- 1/4 cup milk
- 2 cups crushed smoked almonds
- 8 boneless, skinless chicken breasts (4 ounces each), pounded flat
- 6 ounces Brie cheese
- 1/4 cup olive oil

Grated orange peel, for garnish

Bring raspberries, water and honey to a boil in a medium saucepan. Cook over medium heat until raspberries begin to break up, about 3-4 minutes. In a small bowl mix cornstarch with cold water until smooth. Add to raspberries and continue to cook 1 minute longer, stirring constantly. Strain through a fine sieve. Season with salt and pepper to taste. Set aside.

Preheat oven to 350 degrees. Beat eggs and milk in a small bowl. Dip chicken breasts in egg mixture.

Place crushed almonds in a shallow pan. Press each breast into crushed almonds to coat both sides. Cut Brie into eight, 1/4-inch slices; set aside.

Heat oil in a large skillet on medium-high heat. Sauté both sides of breasts until cooked through and golden brown. Place cooked breasts on baking sheet. Top each breast with a slice of Brie cheese. Place in oven and bake until cheese is slightly melted, 1-2 minutes. Place 2 breasts together sandwich-style with cheese in the middle. To serve, top with warm Raspberry Sauce. Garnish with grated orange peel.

Poulet Asperge
with Creamed Brandy Cider Sauce

Yield: 4 servings

Creamed Brandy Cider Sauce:
- 2 tablespoons butter, melted
- 2 tablespoons flour
- 1/4 cup brandy
- 1 cup apple cider
- 1/4 cup heavy whipping cream
- Pinch of cinnamon

- 1/4 cup olive oil
- 4 skinless and boneless chicken breasts, split into halves
- 1/2 cup flour
- 12 asparagus spears, steamed until tender
- 8 slices Brie cheese, cut 3-4 inches long, 1/4-inch thick

To make sauce, combine butter and flour in a small bowl; set aside.

In a small saucepan over high heat, bring brandy to a boil. Touch a lighted match to brandy to create flame. Remove pan from heat and swirl brandy in pan until flames disappear. Return to heat and add cider, cream and cinnamon. Heat to boiling; reduce heat. Slowly add just enough butter and flour mixture to thicken. Simmer 3 minutes, stirring constantly.

Preheat oven to 375 degrees.

Heat oil in a large frying pan on medium-high heat until hot. Dredge chicken breasts in flour and sauté until cooked through and brown on both sides. Place 4 of the halves on a baking sheet. Top each half with 3 asparagus spears and 2 slices of cheese. Cover with remaining 4 pieces of chicken. Bake until cheese barely begins to melt, approximately 3 minutes. Remove from oven and serve topped with warm Creamed Brandy Cider Sauce.

Maple Buttered Roast Chicken

Yield: 4 servings

1/2 cup (1 stick) butter,
     at room temperature
1/2 tablespoon vanilla extract
1/2 teaspoon ground dried ginger
1/2 tablespoon chopped parsley
1/4 teaspoon salt
1/4 teaspoon pepper
  2 tablespoons maple syrup
     Pinch of dried nutmeg (optional)
  1 roasting chicken, wing tips removed
     (about 3-31/2 pounds)

In a small bowl, combine butter, vanilla, ginger, parsley, salt, pepper, maple syrup and nutmeg; blend until well mixed. On a piece of waxed paper, roll butter mixture into a log shape and place in freezer.

Preheat oven to 375 degrees. Place chicken, breast side up, on rack in shallow roasting pan. Using your fingers, push between the skin and flesh of the chicken and gently loosen the breast skin as far back as possible without tearing. Remove butter from freezer and cut into small pieces. Stuff pieces under skin. Roast 1-11/2 hours, or until juice runs clear when punctured.*

*Roasting chicken with butter under the skin will make the chicken appear very dark; some smoking from oven may occur.

Parmesan Pork Tenderloin with Red Onion Confit

Yield: 4 servings

Red Onion Confit:
- 1/2 cup (1 stick) butter
- 2 red onions, halved and sliced
- 1/2 cup sugar
- 3/4 cup red wine vinegar

- 2 pork tenderloins (approximately 13 ounces each)
- 3/4 cup (1 1/2 sticks) butter, melted
- 1/2 cup freshly grated Parmesan cheese

To make confit, melt butter in a large sauté pan. Add onions, sugar and vinegar. Cook over medium heat, stirring often, until liquid is reduced to a syrup-like consistency and onions are tender, about 25-30 minutes. Set aside.

Preheat oven to 400 degrees. Spray a baking sheet with nonstick cooking spray.

Dip each tenderloin in melted butter and roll in cheese; dip again in butter. Place on baking sheet and sprinkle with remaining Parmesan. Bake 25-30 minutes, or until meat thermometer reaches an internal temperature of 140 degrees. Remove from oven and let pork rest 2 minutes. Slice on the diagonal and fan medallions onto plate. Top with warmed Red Onion Confit. Serve immediately.

Rosemary Baked Rack of Lamb

Photo on page 74

Yield: 6 servings

3	frenched lamb racks
1	cup unseasoned bread crumbs
1	bunch (6-8) chopped scallions
1/2	teaspoon chopped garlic
1/2	teaspoon salt
1/2	teaspoon pepper
1/2	teaspoon onion powder
2 1/2	tablespoons fresh or
	1 tablespoon dried rosemary
1	tablespoon olive oil

Preheat oven to 400 degrees. Spray a cookie sheet with nonstick cooking spray. Cut lamb racks into individual rib chops.

Combine bread crumbs, scallions, garlic, salt, pepper, onion powder, rosemary and oil in a food processor; process until fine.

Spray each lamb chop with cooking spray and coat both sides with bread crumb mixture. Place on prepared sheet and bake 10 minutes. Turn chops over and continue baking 5-10 minutes for medium rare.

ENTREES

Stuffed Tenderloin Filet

Yield: 2 servings

Stuffing:
- 1/2 tablespoon butter
- 1 teaspoon dried thyme leaves
- 1 cup chopped green onions
- 1/2 cup sliced shiitake mushrooms
- 1/2 cup shredded smoked Cheddar cheese

- 2 tenderloin filets (about 6-8 ounces each)
- 2 strips smoked bacon

Preheat oven to 375 degrees.

In a medium frying pan, melt butter over medium-high heat. Sauté thyme, onions and mushrooms until soft, approximately 3 minutes. Remove pan from heat; add Cheddar cheese and set aside to cool.

Make a horizontal slit in each tenderloin filet, working knife around to create a deep pocket. Stuff onion mixture into each filet. Wrap filets with bacon and secure with toothpicks. Insert a meat thermometer in filet and bake until desired degree of doneness, approximately 25 minutes for rare. Serve immediately.

Cracked Black Pepper Crusted New York Strip with Whiskey Cream Sauce

Yield: 2 servings

1/4-1/3 cup whole black peppercorns*
   2 New York strip steaks (about 10 ounces each)
   4 tablespoons butter, melted

Whiskey Cream Sauce:
   2 ounces whiskey
   1 cup heavy whipping cream
   3 tablespoons Worcestershire sauce
     Salt

In a blender or food processor, process peppercorns on high setting until finely crushed, approximately 15 seconds. Roll steaks in peppercorns, pressing pepper into steak with palm of hand. Melt butter in a medium frying pan and sauté steaks to desired doneness, about 5-7 minutes per side. Remove pan from heat, reserving juices. Place cooked steaks in a warm serving dish.

To make sauce, place pan with reserved meat juices over medium heat. Add whiskey, whipping cream and Worcestershire; reduce mixture until thick, approximately 5-8 minutes. Season with salt to taste. To serve, pour warm sauce over steaks and serve immediately.

*Adjust peppercorns to individual taste.

Note: Sauté steaks in a well-ventilated cooking area as pepper crusted steaks will produce smoke.

DESSERTS

Door County Cherry Pie

Photo on page 76

Yield: 8 servings

Crust:
- 2 1/2 cups flour
- 1 tablespoon sugar
- 1 cup lard
- 4-5 tablespoons ice water

Filling:
- 4 cups pitted, fresh or frozen tart Montmorency cherries*
- 1/4 teaspoon almond extract
- 1 1/4 cups sugar
- 1 1/2 tablespoons cornstarch

Preheat oven to 425 degrees.

Combine flour and sugar in a large bowl. Cut in lard with a pastry blender until dough begins to stick together. Add ice water, one tablespoon at a time, and toss with a fork until all flour is moistened and pastry forms a slightly sticky ball. Divide dough in half and pat into 2 rounds. On a lightly floured surface, roll dough to 2 inches larger than an inverted 9-inch pie plate. Place 1 round in bottom of pie plate.

To make filling, combine cherries and almond extract in a medium bowl. In a separate bowl, stir together sugar and cornstarch. Gently toss sugar mixture into cherries to combine. Pour filling over prepared crust and cover with top crust. Pinch edges and seal; trim excess dough. Cut several slits in top crust to allow steam to escape. Bake 35-45 minutes, or until crust is golden brown and filling is bubbly.

*If using frozen cherries, drain and reserve 1/4 cup juice. Combine cherries and reserved juice.

Montmorency Cherry Almond Pie

Yield: 8 servings

>   5   cups pitted, tart Montmorency cherries with juice
>   1/2   teaspoon almond extract
>   5   tablespoons cornstarch
>   1/2   cup sugar
>   1   teaspoon cinnamon
>   1   prebaked 9-inch deep dish pie shell

Topping:
>   1/4   cup plus 2 tablespoons flour
>   1/4   cup sugar
>   1/4   cup (1/2 stick) cold butter, cut in pieces
>   1/4   cup plus 2 tablespoons shredded coconut
>   1/4   cup sliced almonds

Preheat oven to 350 degrees.

In a medium saucepan, heat cherries, almond extract, cornstarch, sugar and cinnamon over low to medium heat until mixture becomes thick and clear. Cool slightly. Pour into prepared pie shell; set aside.

With pastry cutter, mix flour, sugar and butter until crumbs are formed. Stir in coconut and almonds. Sprinkle topping over pie. Bake 45 minutes, or until topping is golden brown. Cover edges of pie crust with aluminum foil if browning too quickly. Remove pie from oven and cool slightly before serving.

French Silk Pie

Yield: 10 servings

1	cup (2 sticks) butter, softened
1 1/2	cups sugar
4	packets Choco Bake*
2	teaspoons vanilla extract
2/3	cup pasteurized eggs or equivalent of 4 eggs**
1	prebaked 9-inch pie crust, thoroughly cooled
	Whipped cream, for garnish
	Shaved chocolate, for garnish

In a large bowl, cream together butter and sugar until light and fluffy. Blend in Choco Bake and vanilla. Add eggs gradually, beating well. Pour chocolate mixture into prepared pie crust. Chill at least 2 hours prior to serving. Garnish with whipped cream and shaved chocolate.

*Available in the baking section of most supermarkets.

**Available at specialty food and larger grocery stores. Pasteurized eggs are recommended whenever eggs are not going to be thoroughly cooked.

Apple Dumplings
with Brandy Cream Sauce

Photo on page 76

Yield: 6 dumplings

3 frozen puff pastry sheets, (9 x 9 inches each), thawed
6 medium size tart baking apples, cored and peeled
1/3 cup granulated sugar
1/3 cup chopped pecans
2 tablespoons butter, softened
Milk

Brandy Cream Sauce:
1/2 cup brown sugar
2 tablespoons butter
1/2 cup heavy whipping cream
11/2 tablespoons brandy
Dash cinnamon

Preheat oven to 375 degrees F.

Lay out sheets of puff pastry. Trim a two-inch strip from one side of each sheet of pastry to form 9 x 7-inch rectangles. Set trimmed strips aside. Cut each rectangle in half to create six 41/2 x 7-inch rectangles. Place an apple in the center of each. In a small bowl, stir together sugar, pecans and butter. Stuff 11/2 tablespoons of the mixture in the center of each apple. Fold pastry up around each apple, sealing seams well and twisting the top to create a "stem." If desired, decorate apples with leaf shapes cut from trimmed pastry and pressed onto dumplings. Place dumplings on a baking sheet. Brush with milk and bake 35-45 minutes until apples are fork tender and pastry is golden brown.

While dumplings are baking, combine brown sugar, butter, cream, brandy and cinnamon in a heavy saucepan. Cook over medium heat, stirring often until mixture comes to a boil, 3-4 minutes. Serve sauce over warm dumplings.

White Chocolate Coconut Cake

Yield: 12 servings

4 ounces white chocolate,
   chopped
1/2 cup heavy whipping cream
1/2 cup (1 stick) butter, softened
1 cup sugar
1 teaspoon vanilla extract
3 large eggs
2 cups flour

1 teaspoon baking soda
1/4 teaspoon salt
2/3 cup buttermilk

Frosting:
2 cups flaked sweetened coconut,
   divided
2 cups heavy whipping cream
1/4 cup sugar

Preheat oven to 350 degrees. Spray two 8-inch round pans with nonstick cooking spray and lightly dust with flour.

Place chocolate and whipping cream in top pan of double boiler. Cook over low heat until chocolate is melted; whisk until smooth and set aside.

Using an electric mixer, cream together butter and sugar in a large bowl until light and fluffy, approximately 3 minutes. Add vanilla. Add eggs, one at a time, beating well after each addition. Add cooled chocolate mixture and beat at low speed until well blended.

In a medium bowl, stir together flour, baking soda and salt. Add alternately with buttermilk to batter, beginning and ending with flour mixture. Beat until smooth. Divide batter between pans and bake 30-40 minutes, or until top is slightly brown and a wooden pick inserted in center comes out clean. Remove from oven and cool completely before removing cake from pans.

To make frosting, place 1/4 cup of the coconut in a food processor and process to a fine dust; set aside. In a medium bowl, beat chilled whipping cream with sugar until mixture forms stiff peaks. Gently fold in coconut dust. Spread frosting between cooled layers, around sides and on top of cake. Press remaining 13/4 cups coconut into the whipped cream frosting. Refrigerate until serving.

Double Chocolate Cheesecake

Yield: 10-12 servings

Crust:
- 2 cups finely crushed chocolate wafers (approximately 38 cookies)
- 6 tablespoons butter, melted

Filling:
- 1 bag (16 ounces) semisweet chocolate chips
- 1/2 cup heavy whipping cream
- 3 packages (8 ounces each) cream cheese, at room temperature
- 3/4 cup sugar
- 1 teaspoon vanilla extract
- 4 eggs
  Whipped cream, for garnish
  Shaved chocolate, for garnish

Preheat oven to 300 degrees.

In a medium bowl, combine wafers and melted butter. Press mixture into bottom and partly up sides of a 9-inch springform pan; set aside.

Place chocolate chips and whipping cream in top pan of double boiler. Cook over low heat until chips are melted. Stir until well combined; set aside to cool.

While chocolate is cooling, beat cream cheese, sugar and vanilla in a large bowl until smooth. Gradually add cooled chocolate to cream cheese mixture and blend well. Add eggs one at a time, beating after each addition. Pour over prepared crust and bake 70-80 minutes. (Center may appear moist.) Remove from oven and cool on wire rack at room temperature. Cover with plastic wrap and refrigerate overnight.

To serve, garnish with whipped cream and shaved chocolate, if desired.

White Chocolate Cheesecake with Raspberry Sauce

Yield: 12 servings

Crust:
- 6 tablespoons chilled butter, cubed
- 1 cup plus 2 tablespoons flour
- 2 tablespoons sugar
- 1 large egg yolk
- 1 tablespoon plus 1 teaspoon cold water

Chocolate ganache layer:
- 9 ounces bittersweet chocolate, chopped into small pieces
- 3/4 cup heavy whipping cream

White chocolate filling:
- 19 ounces white chocolate, chopped into small pieces
- 11 tablespoons butter, softened
- 3/4 cup sugar
- 3 packages (8 ounces each) cream cheese, softened
- 2 teaspoons dark rum

Raspberry Sauce:
- 1/3 cup sugar
- 1 package (10 ounces) unsweetened frozen raspberries, thawed and undrained
- 1 tablespoon cold water
- 1 1/2 teaspoons cornstarch

Preheat oven to 350 degrees.

Using a food processor or pastry blender, cut butter into flour and sugar. Add egg yolk and cold water; process until well combined. Press mixture into bottom of an ungreased 9-inch springform pan. Bake 20 minutes. Remove from oven and cool completely.

(continued on page 115)

DESSERTS

While crust is cooling, melt bittersweet chocolate and whipping cream together in the top pan of a double boiler; stir until smooth. Spread over cooled crust and chill.

In the top pan of a double boiler, melt white chocolate until it becomes a soft mass; set aside. In a large mixing bowl, beat butter until creamy with electric mixer on medium speed. Add sugar and continue beating 2-3 minutes. Scrape down sides of bowl and add cream cheese, one third at a time. Beat in rum. Slowly beat in softened white chocolate; increase speed and beat until creamy. Pour over chocolate ganache layer and gently spread to edge of pan. Cover with plastic wrap and refrigerate overnight.

To make sauce, bring sugar and raspberries to a boil in a heavy saucepan, stirring often. Mix together water and cornstarch; stir into raspberries. Return mixture to a boil and cook for 1 minute, stirring constantly. Remove from heat and cool.

Serve individual pieces of cheesecake topped with Raspberry Sauce.

Note: Cake can be frozen for up to 5 days. Thaw in refrigerator before serving.

Crème de Menthe Cheesecake

Yield: 10-12 servings

Crust:
- 2 cups finely crushed chocolate wafers (approximately 38 cookies)
- 6 tablespoons butter, melted

Filling:
- 3 packages (8 ounces each) cream cheese, at room temperature
- 1 cup sugar
- 4 eggs
- 1/3 cup green crème de menthe
- 1 teaspoon vanilla extract
- Hot fudge, for topping
- Whipped cream, for topping
- Sprigs of fresh mint, for garnish

Preheat oven to 375 degrees.

In a medium bowl, combine wafers and melted butter; mix well. Press mixture into bottom and partially up sides of a 9-inch springform pan.

Beat cream cheese with sugar in a large bowl. Add eggs, one at a time, beating well after each addition. Stir in crème de menthe and vanilla. Pour filling into prepared crust.

Bake 55-60 minutes, or until a knife inserted in center comes out clean. Cool on a wire rack at room temperature. Chill at least 4-5 hours, preferably overnight before serving.

To serve, run a knife around rim of cake to loosen sides from pan. Top individual slices with hot fudge and whipped cream and garnish with a sprig of fresh mint.

DESSERTS

Peppermint Cheesecake

Yield: 12 servings

Crust:
- 2 cups chocolate wafer crumbs (approximately 38 cookies)
- 6 tablespoons butter, melted

Filling:
- 1 envelope unflavored gelatin
- 1/4 cup cold water
- 2 packages (8 ounces each) cream cheese, softened
- 1/2 cup sugar
- 1/2 cup milk
- 1/3 cup crushed peppermint hard candies (approximately 11)
- 1 cup heavy whipping cream
- 2 bars (1.55 ounces each) milk chocolate candy, finely chopped
  Whipped cream, for garnish
  Shaved chocolate, for garnish

Preheat oven to 350 degrees.

In a medium bowl, stir together chocolate wafer crumbs and melted butter. Press mixture into bottom of an ungreased 9-inch springform pan. Bake 15 minutes. Remove pan from oven and cool completely.

In a small saucepan, stir gelatin into cold water to soften. Cook over low heat until gelatin dissolves; set aside.

In a large bowl, beat together cream cheese and sugar until well blended. Gradually add gelatin, milk and peppermint candy, mixing until blended. Chill until slightly thickened.

While cream cheese mixture is chilling, whip cream in a medium bowl. Fold whipped cream and chopped chocolate into cream cheese mixture and pour over cooled crust. Chill until firm and garnish with additional whipped cream and shaved chocolate. Cake can be frozen for up to 5 days. Thaw in refrigerator before serving.

DESSERTS

Blackberry Custard Torte

Yield: 12 servings

Cake:
- 4 ounces white chocolate, chopped
- 1/2 cup heavy whipping cream
- 1/2 cup (1 stick) butter, softened
- 1 cup sugar
- 1 teaspoon vanilla extract
- 3 large eggs
- 2 cups flour
- 1 teaspoon baking soda
- 1/4 teaspoon salt
- 2/3 cup buttermilk

Custard:
- 5 egg yolks
- 11/2 cups milk
- 1/2 cup sugar
- 11/2 tablespoons cornstarch
- 1 teaspoon vanilla extract

Frosting:
- 2 cups heavy whipping cream
- 1/4 cup sugar
- 1/4 cup grated white chocolate

2 cups fresh blackberries

Preheat oven to 350 degrees. Spray two 8-inch round cake pans with non-stick cooking spray and lightly dust with flour.

Slowly melt chocolate and whipping cream together in the top pan of a double boiler. Whisk until smooth; set aside.

In a large bowl, cream together butter and sugar until light and fluffy, approximately 3 minutes. Add vanilla. Add eggs, one at a time, beating well after each addition. Add cooled chocolate mixture and beat with electric mixer on low speed until well blended.

In a medium bowl, stir together flour, baking soda and salt. Add alternately with buttermilk to cake batter, beginning and ending with flour mixture. Beat until smooth. Divide batter between prepared pans and bake 30-40 minutes, or until top is slightly brown and a wooden pick inserted in center comes out clean. Cool cake completely before removing from pans.

(continued on page 119)

DESSERTS

To make custard, combine egg yolks, milk, sugar and cornstarch in a heavy saucepan and cook over low heat until mixture reaches 150 degrees, stirring constantly, until thickened. Remove pan from heat and stir in vanilla. Cover with plastic wrap and chill completely.

While cake and custard are cooling, make frosting by whipping together whipping cream and sugar until mixture forms stiff peaks. Gently fold in grated white chocolate.

To assemble torte, carefully slice cake layers in half horizontally, forming 4 layers. Spread one third of the custard over first layer and sprinkle with one third of the berries. Continue in the same manner with the second and third layers. Place the fourth layer on top, frosting top and sides with whipped cream frosting. Refrigerate until serving.

D E S S E R T S

Poppy Seed Torte

Yield: 12 servings

Cake:
- 1/3 cup poppy seeds
- 3/4 cup milk
- 3/4 cup (1 1/2 sticks) butter, softened
- 1 1/2 cups sugar
- 1 3/4 cups flour
- 2 1/2 teaspoons baking powder
- 1 teaspoon salt
- 5 egg whites
- 1 1/2 teaspoons vanilla extract

Filling:
- 1/2 cup sugar
- 1 tablespoon cornstarch
- 1 1/2 cups milk
- 5 egg yolks, slightly beaten
- 1 teaspoon vanilla extract

Frosting:
- 3/4 cup sugar
- 1 1/2 cups heavy whipping cream

Preheat oven to 375 degrees. Line two 9-inch round cake pans with waxed paper and spray with nonstick cooking spray.

Soak poppy seeds in milk for 1 hour in a small bowl. Cream together butter and sugar in a large mixing bowl. In a separate bowl, sift together flour, baking powder and salt.

In a medium bowl, whip egg whites until stiff; set aside.

Add vanilla to poppy seeds and milk. Alternately add dry ingredients and poppy seed mixture to butter and sugar; mix until well combined. Gently fold in beaten egg whites. Bake in prepared pans 30-35 minutes, or until knife inserted in center comes out clean. Cool cakes 10 minutes in pans. Remove from pans and cool completely on wire rack.

(continued on page 121)

Meanwhile, combine sugar and cornstarch in a heavy saucepan. Add milk and egg yolks; cook over medium heat to a temperature of 150 degrees, stirring constantly until bubbly. Continue to cook 1 minute longer. Remove from heat and stir in vanilla. Cover with plastic wrap and refrigerate until completely cooled.

Split each cake layer in half horizontally. Position bottom layer on cake plate and spread with one third of custard filling. Add additional layers and custard. Place final layer of cake on top.

To make frosting, whip sugar and whipping cream together in a small bowl until mixture reaches spreading consistency. Spread over sides and top of cake. Refrigerate cake until serving.

Go Nuts Tart

Yield: 12 servings

1/2 cup (1 stick) butter, softened
1/2 cup granulated sugar
  2 cups flour
  1 tablespoon ice water
3/4 cup whole or coarsely chopped unsalted walnuts
3/4 cup whole or coarsely chopped unsalted pecans
3/4 cup whole or coarsely chopped unsalted macadamia nuts
3/4 cup whole or coarsely chopped unsalted almonds
3/4 cup whole or coarsely chopped unsalted cashews

Caramel sauce:
  1 cup (2 sticks) butter
11/2 cups heavy whipping cream
13/4 cups brown sugar

Preheat oven to 375 degrees. Spray a 9-inch pie pan or tart pan with non-stick cooking spray.

Mix together butter, sugar, flour and ice water by hand with pastry blender or in food processor until dough begins to form; press into pan. Set aside.

Combine walnuts, pecans, macadamias, almonds and cashews in a large bowl; stir to mix. Sprinkle evenly over crust; set aside.

In a heavy saucepan, heat butter, whipping cream and brown sugar over medium heat until butter is melted and sugar is dissolved, approximately 10-15 minutes. Pour hot caramel sauce over nuts. Place pan on a baking sheet and position in center of oven. Bake 25-30 minutes. Remove from oven and allow to cool. Refrigerate at least 2 hours before serving.

Note: To easily remove tart from pan before serving, set in a warm oven for 1 or 2 minutes.

Crème Brûlée

Yield: 6 servings

5 egg yolks
1/4 cup granulated sugar
2 cups heavy whipping cream
1 teaspoon vanilla extract
2 tablespoons brown sugar
  Fresh fruit, for garnish

Preheat oven to 350 degrees.

Whisk together egg yolks and granulated sugar in a medium bowl; set aside.

In a small heavy saucepan, heat cream over medium-high setting to just below boiling point. Remove from heat. Add a small amount of hot cream to egg mixture; mix well. Slowly add remaining cream and vanilla; stir until well combined. Pour mixture into six, 4-ounce custard cups. Place custard cups in a 13 x 9-inch baking pan. Pour hot water into pan to within 1/2-inch of tops of cups, being careful not to spill any water into cups. Bake 45-50 minutes. Remove pan from oven and cups from pan. Refrigerate cups for at least 2 hours.

Just before serving, turn oven to broil setting. Sprinkle 1 teaspoon brown sugar over each custard and place under broiler, approximately four inches from heat. Broil 3-4 minutes, or until sugar has caramelized. Spoon fresh fruit over top and serve immediately.

DESSERTS

Truffle Trio Torte

Photo on page 76

Yield: 24 servings

Cake:
- 6 ounces bittersweet chocolate, chopped
- 4 1/2 tablespoons butter
- 4 large eggs, separated
- 3 1/2 tablespoons sugar, divided
- 1 tablespoon flour

Milk chocolate truffle layer:
- 16 ounces milk chocolate, chopped
- 3/4 cup heavy whipping cream
- 1 tablespoon Grand Marnier liqueur

White chocolate truffle layer:
- 16 ounces white chocolate, chopped
- 3/4 cup heavy whipping cream
- 1 tablespoon hazelnut liqueur

Bittersweet chocolate truffle layer:
- 16 ounces bittersweet chocolate, chopped
- 3/4 cup heavy whipping cream
- 1 tablespoon maple syrup

Mint sprigs, for garnish
Powdered sugar, for garnish

Preheat oven to 350 degrees.

To make cake, melt bittersweet chocolate with butter in a heavy saucepan or top pan of a double boiler; cool slightly. In a separate bowl, beat egg yolks with 1 1/2 tablespoons of the sugar until pale, approximately 2-3 minutes. Gradually add melted chocolate to beaten egg yolks and beat until shiny. Sprinkle flour over mixture but do not stir in.

In a separate bowl, beat egg whites and gradually add remaining 2 tablespoons sugar; beat until glossy. Gently fold egg whites into chocolate mixture

(continued on page 125)

and pour into an ungreased 8-inch springform pan. Bake 20-25 minutes. Remove from oven and set aside to cool.

When cake has cooled, slide knife around sides of pan to loosen cake. Remove springform ring and slice cake in half horizontally. Remove top half and set aside. Reassemble springform pan around bottom half of cake. In the top pan of a double boiler, melt milk chocolate with whipping cream; stir until smooth. Remove from heat and add Grand Marnier; cool slightly. Pour milk chocolate mixture over cake in springform pan. Place in freezer until chocolate has set, at least 2 hours.

While milk chocolate is setting, melt white chocolate and whipping cream together in the top pan of a double boiler; stir until smooth. Remove from heat and add hazelnut liqueur; cool slightly. Pour white chocolate mixture over milk chocolate layer and return to freezer for 2 hours.

Melt bittersweet chocolate and whipping cream together in the top pan of a double boiler; stir until smooth. Remove from heat and add maple syrup. Pour over white chocolate layer. Immediately cover with reserved cake layer. Return to freezer for at least 2 more hours. After 2 hours, transfer to refrigerator and allow to sit overnight.

To remove torte from pan, run heated knife around the outside rim and loosen sides of springform pan. Serve garnished with a sprig of mint or a dusting of powdered sugar.

Key Lime
White Chocolate Triangles

Yield: 12 servings

Crust:
- 1/2 cup (1 stick) butter, softened
- 1/4 cup sugar
- 1 large egg yolk
- 1 cup plus 2 tablespoons flour

Key lime filling:
- 3 cups sweetened condensed milk
- 3 large egg yolks
- 3/4 cup key lime juice

White chocolate ganache:
- 3 tablespoons milk
- 3 tablespoons heavy whipping cream
- 12 ounces white chocolate
- 3/4 teaspoon light rum

Shaved white chocolate, for garnish
Lime zest, for garnish

Preheat oven to 350 degrees.

In a medium bowl, cream together butter and sugar with an electric mixer. Add egg yolk and beat 1 minute more. Reduce speed to low and gradually beat in flour until just incorporated. Press mixture into bottom of an ungreased 9-inch springform pan and bake 10-15 minutes. Remove pan from oven and cool completely.

In a medium bowl, beat together sweetened condensed milk and egg yolks until smooth. Slowly add lime juice and beat until well combined. Pour mixture over crust and bake until set, 25-30 minutes. Remove pan from oven and allow to cool slightly at room temperature. Transfer to refrigerator and chill several hours. After chilling, run a knife around torte and remove outside ring of springform pan. Cut torte into 12 slices and transfer to a flat baking sheet.

(continued on page 127)

To make ganache, in the top pan of a double boiler, heat milk, whipping cream and white chocolate When chocolate has melted, remove from heat and stir in rum. Allow mixture to cool slightly. Carefully spoon ganache over key lime triangles, covering completely. Place triangles in refrigerator for several hours. Before serving, trim away excess ganache which has pooled around triangles. Serve garnished with shaved white chocolate and lime zest.

Rhubarb Torte

Yield: 6-8 servings

Crust:
- 1 cup flour
- Pinch of salt
- 5 tablespoons powdered sugar
- 1/2 cup (1 stick) butter, softened

Filling:
- 2 eggs
- 1 1/2 cups granulated sugar
- 1/4 cup flour
- 3 cups diced rhubarb

Whipped cream or vanilla ice cream

Preheat oven to 350 degrees.

Combine flour, salt and powdered sugar in a medium bowl. Using a pastry blender, cut in butter until mixture is the size of small peas. Press into a 9 x 9-inch glass baking dish and bake 12 minutes. Remove from oven and allow to cool slightly.

Meanwhile, in a large bowl, beat eggs with a fork. Add granulated sugar and flour; beat well. Arrange rhubarb evenly over crust. Top with egg mixture and bake 50-55 minutes, or until top begins to brown. To serve, top with whipped cream or vanilla ice cream.

Macadamia Nut Tarts with Grand Marnier Sauce

Photo on page 76

Yield: 6 servings

3/4 cup (1 1/2 sticks) butter
1/2 cup sugar
2 cups coarsely chopped macadamia nuts
1 tablespoon grated orange rind
1/4 cup heavy whipping cream

Crust:
1/4 cup sugar
1 cup flour
1/4 cup (1/2 stick) butter, chilled
1 tablespoon ice water

Whipped cream
Grand Marnier Sauce

Preheat oven to 350 degrees. Spray six 3-inch tart pans* with nonstick cooking spray.

Melt butter in a heavy saucepan. Add sugar and bring mixture to a boil. Stir in nuts, orange zest and whipping cream. Return to a boil, stirring constantly. Remove from heat and set aside.

To make crust, combine sugar and flour in a medium bowl. Cut in butter with a pastry blender until mixture is the size of small peas. Add ice water and mix until just combined. Press a thin layer of crust mixture into the bottom and up the sides of each tart pan. Spoon nut mixture into pans until three-quarters full. Bake approximately 15 minutes, or until filling is bubbly. Remove from oven and cool completely. To remove tarts from pan, run a thin knife around sides to loosen. Serve topped with whipped cream and Grand Marnier Sauce (page 129).

*If tart pans are not available, muffin tins may be substituted.

DESSERTS

Grand Marnier Sauce

Yield: 2 cups

1/2 cup Grand Marnier
2 cups water
1/2 cup sugar
1 tablespoon orange zest
2 1/2 teaspoons cornstarch

In a heavy saucepan, combine Grand Marnier, water, sugar, orange zest and cornstarch. Cook over medium-high heat and bring to a boil, stirring constantly. Boil 1 minute. Remove from heat and serve warm over Macadamia Nut Tarts (page 128).

Double Chocolate Cookies

Yield: 2 1/2 dozen cookies

1	cup (2 sticks) butter, softened
11/2	cups sugar
2	eggs
1	teaspoon vanilla extract
21/4	cups flour
3/4	cup unsweetened cocoa
3/4	teaspoon baking soda
1	cup semisweet chocolate chips

Preheat oven to 375 degrees.

Using an electric mixer on high, cream together butter, sugar, eggs and vanilla in a medium bowl.

In a separate bowl, mix together flour, cocoa and baking soda. Stir into creamed mixture. Add chocolate chips. Drop by rounded teaspoonfuls onto an ungreased cookie sheet. Flatten cookies slightly with spatula. Bake 10-12 minutes. Cool slightly; remove from cookie sheet. Store in airtight container.

Farmer Cookies

Yield: 4 dozen cookies

3/4 cup granulated sugar
1 cup brown sugar
1 cup (2 sticks) butter, softened
2 eggs
2 cups flour
1 teaspoon baking soda
1/2 teaspoon salt
1 teaspoon cinnamon
1 cup chocolate chips
1 cup chopped pecans
1 cup shredded, sweetened coconut
1 cup raisins
2 cups oatmeal

Preheat oven to 375 degrees. Using an electric mixer on high, cream together granulated sugar, brown sugar, butter and eggs in a large bowl.

In a separate bowl, combine flour, baking soda, salt and cinnamon. Add to creamed mixture. Stir in chocolate chips, pecans, coconut, raisins and oatmeal. Drop dough by rounded teaspoonfuls, about 2 inches apart, onto ungreased cookie sheets. Bake 10-12 minutes, or until lightly browned. Cool slightly; remove from cookie sheet. Store in airtight container.

Maple Oatmeal Cookies

Yield: 6 dozen cookies

1 1/2　cups (3 sticks) butter, softened
1 1/2　cups Door County maple syrup
1　cup sugar
2　large eggs
2 1/2　teaspoons vanilla extract
6　cups old-fashioned rolled oats
2　cups flour
2　teaspoons baking soda
1/2　teaspoon salt

Preheat oven to 350 degrees. Spray two baking sheets with nonstick cooking spray.

In a large bowl, with an electric mixer, beat together butter, maple syrup, sugar, eggs and vanilla. Stir in oats. In a separate bowl, stir together flour, baking soda and salt. Add dry ingredients to creamed mixture and mix well. Drop by rounded teaspoonfuls about 2 inches apart on prepared baking sheets and bake 12-15 minutes.

INDEX

INDEX

Page numbers for color photographs of dishes are in *bold italics*.

A

Alaskan Crab Cakes 84
APPETIZERS
    Alaskan Crab Cakes 84
    Baked Brie and Fruit
       in Puff Pastry 88
    Braised Black Beans 85
    Buckwheat Scones with
       Smoked Salmon and
       Cream Cheese 89
    Herbed Spinach Cakes 90
    Pineapple Salsa 85
    Roasted Red Bell Pepper
       Sauce 87
    Scallops in Puff Pastry with
       Roasted Red Bell Pepper
       Sauce 86
Apple Dumplings with Brandy
    Cream Sauce *76*, 111
Award Winning 3-Bean
    Chicken Chili 49

B

Baked Brie and Fruit
    in Puff Pastry 88
Banana Walnut Muffins. 33
Bean(s)
    Chicken Chili, Award
       Winning. 49
    Braised Black 85
    Soup, Black. 46
Beef
    New York Strip,
       Cracked Black Pepper
       Crusted with Whiskey Cream
       Sauce 106

    Soup, Hearty Barley 40
    Tenderloin Filet, Stuffed . . . 105
Biscuits, Buttermilk
    with Sausage Gravy. 28
Black Bean Soup 46
Blackberry Custard Torte. 118
Blueberry Bread. 37
Braised Black Beans. 85
Bran Muffins with
    Cream Cheese Filling 34
Buckwheat Scones with Smoked
    Salmon and Cream Cheese . . 89
BREADS
    Banana Walnut Muffins 33
    Blueberry Bread. 37
    Bran Muffins with
       Cream Cheese Filling. 34
    Candlelight Dinner
       Tied Rolls 36
    Lemon Bread 37
    Maple Pecan Scones
       with Maple Butter 35
    Morning Cinnamon
       Rolls. 32, *72*
    Steve's Swedish Limpa
       Bread 38
BREAKFAST & BRUNCH
    Breakfast Rice Pudding 24
    Buttermilk Biscuits
       with Sausage Gravy 28
    Cherry and Cream Cheese
       Stuffed French Toast. . . 21, *72*
    Cherry Pancakes 22
    Crab, Artichoke Heart and
       Cream Cheese Quiche 30
    Door County Omelet Filling. . 26
    French Canadian Quiche. . . . 29
    Montmorency Cherry Coffee
       Cake. 20, *71*

INDEX

Omelet Olé Filling 27
Turkey Hash Browns
  with Dijon Gravy 25
White Gull Inn Granola. . 23, 72
Breakfast Rice Pudding 24
Broccoli Salad 66
Buckwheat Scones with
  Smoked Salmon and
  Cream Cheese. 89
Burgundy Mushroom Soup 43
Buttermilk Biscuits
  with Sausage Gravy 28

C

Cake, White Chocolate
  Coconut 112
Candlelight Dinner Tied Rolls . . 36
Cheesecake
  Double Chocolate 113
  Crème de Menthe 116
  Peppermint 117
  White Chocolate
    with Raspberry Sauce 114
Cherry
  Coffee Cake,
    Montmorency 20, 71
  French Toast, Cream Cheese
    Stuffed and. 21
  Pancakes 22, 71
  Pie, Door County 76, 108
  Pie, Montmorency Almond. . 109
  Soup, Door County Chilled
    with Cinnamon Croutons. . 52
Cherry and Cream Cheese
  Stuffed French Toast 21, 72
Cherry Pancakes 22, 71
Chicken
  3-Bean Chili,
    Award Winning 49
  Asperge, with Creamed
    Brandy Cider Sauce 101

Raspberry Amandine . . . 75, 100
Roast, Maple Buttered 102
Salad, Curried Rice 65
Salad, Grilled with
  Honey Lime Dressing. . 62, 73
Soup, Almond 50
Chicken Almond Soup 50
Chili, Award Winning 3-Bean. . 49
Chocolate
  Cake, White Coconut 112
  Cheesecake, Double. 113
  Cheesecake, White with
    Raspberry Sauce 114
  Cookies, Double 130
  Pie, French Silk. 110
  Torte, Truffle Trio 124
  Triangles, Key Lime White. . 126
Cinnamon Croutons 53
Coffee Cake,
  Montmorency Cherry 20
Cookies
  Double Chocolate 130
  Farmer 131
  Maple Oatmeal 132
Crab, Alaskan Cakes 84
Crab, Artichoke Heart
  and Cream Cheese Quiche . . 30
Crabmeat and Wild Rice
  Salad 63, 73
Cracked Black Pepper Crusted
  New York Strip with
  Whiskey Cream Sauce. 106
Cream of Garlic and Onion
  Soup 41
Cream of Mushroom with
  Wild Rice Soup. 42
Cream of Winter Squash Soup . . 45
Creamy Parmesan Cracked
  Peppercorn Dressing 59
Crème Brûlée 123
Crème de Menthe
  Cheesecake 116
Croutons, Cinnamon 53

INDEX

Cucumber Dill Sauce. 81

Curried Chicken Rice Salad. . . . 65

D

DESSERTS

Apple Dumplings with Brandy
Cream Sauce. *76*, 111

Blackberry Custard Torte. . . 118

Crème Brûlée 123

Crème de Menthe
Cheesecake. 116

Door County
Cherry Pie *76*, 108

Double Chocolate
Cheesecake. 113

Double Chocolate Cookies. . 130

Farmer Cookies. 131

French Silk Pie 110

Go Nuts Tart. 122

Grand Marnier Sauce 129

Key Lime White Chocolate
Triangles. 126

Macadamia Nut Tarts with
Grand Marnier Sauce. . *76*, 128

Maple Oatmeal Cookies . . . 132

Montmorency Cherry
Almond Pie 109

Peppermint Cheesecake. . . . 117

Poppy Seed Torte 120

Rhubarb Torte. 127

Truffle Trio Torte. *76*, 124

White Chocolate Cheesecake
with Raspberry Sauce 114

White Chocolate Coconut
Cake. 112

Door County Cherry Pie . . *76*, 108

Door County Chilled Cherry
Soup with Cinnamon
Croutons. 52

Door County Omelet Filling . . . 26

Double Chocolate
Cheesecake 113

Double Chocolate Cookies . . . 130

DRESSINGS

Creamy Parmesan Cracked
Peppercorn 59

French. 57

Honey Lime 56

Maple Syrup and Balsamic
Vinegar 60

Raspberry Vinaigrette 56

Roasted Pecan Roquefort. . . . 58

E

ENTREES

Cracked Black Pepper Crusted
New York Strip with
Whiskey Cream Sauce . . . 106

Hollandaise Sauce 97

Macadamia Crusted Salmon
with Lime Ginger Butter . . 92

Maple Buttered Roast
Chicken 102

Oriental Pan-Seared
Sea Scallops 94

Parmesan Pork Tenderloin with
Red Onion Confit 103

Poulet Asperge with Creamed
Brandy Cider Sauce 101

Raspberry Chicken
Amandine. *75*, 100

Rosemary Baked
Rack of Lamb. *74*, 104

Shrimp and Artichoke
Romano 93

Stuffed Tenderloin Filet. . . . 105

White Gull Inn Fish Boil . . . 98

Whitefish Oscar with
Hollandaise Sauce. 96

Whitefish Parmesan 99

Wisconsin Walleye
au Gratin 95

INDEX

F

Farmer Cookies 131
Fish and Seafood
    Crab Cakes, Alaskan 84
    Crabmeat and Wild Rice
      Salad 63
    Fish Boil, White Gull Inn . . . 98
    Salmon, Macadamia Crusted
      with Lime Ginger Butter . . 92
    Salmon, Smoked with
      Buckwheat Scones 89
    Scallops in Puff Pastry with
      Roasted Red Bell Pepper
      Sauce 86
    Sea Scallops,
      Oriental Pan-Seared 94
    Shrimp and Artichoke
      Romano 93
    Walleye, Wisconsin
      au Gratin 95
    Whitefish Oscar with
      Hollandaise Sauce 96
    Whitefish Parmesan 99
French Canadian Quiche 29
French Dressing 57
French Silk Pie 110
French Toast, Cherry and
    Cream Cheese Stuffed . . . 21, *72*

G

Garden Sandwich with
    Cucumber Dill Sauce 80
Gazpacho Soup 54
Go Nuts Tart 122
Grand Marnier Sauce 129
Granola, White Gull Inn . . . 23, *72*
Grilled Chicken Salad with
    Honey Lime Dressing . . . 62, *73*

H

Hearty Beef Barley Soup 40
Herbed Spinach Cakes 90
Hollandaise Sauce 97
Honey Dijon Sauce 78
Honey Lime Dressing 56

I

Italian Vegetable Soup 48

K

Key Lime White Chocolate
    Triangles 126

L

Lamb, Rosemary Baked
    Rack of *74*, 104
Lemon Bread 37

M

Macadamia Nut Tarts with
    Grand Marnier Sauce . . . *76*, 128
Macadamia Crusted Salmon
    with Lime Ginger Butter 92
Maple
    Chicken, Buttered Roast . . . 102
    Cookies, Oatmeal 132
    Dressing, Syrup and
      Balsamic Vinegar 60
    Scones, Pecan with
      Maple Butter 35
Maple Buttered Roast
    Chicken 102

INDEX

Maple Oatmeal Cookies 132
Maple Pecan Scones
    with Maple Butter. 35
Maple Syrup and Balsamic
    Vinegar Dressing. 60
Montmorency Cherry
    Almond Pie. 109
Montmorency Cherry
    Coffee Cake 20, *71*
Morning Cinnamon Rolls . . 32, *72*
Muffins, Banana Walnut 33
Muffins, Bran with
    Cream Cheese Filling 34

O

Omelet, Door County Filling . . 26
Omelet Olé Filling 27
Open Doorwich with
    Honey Dijon Sauce *73*, 78
Oriental Pan-Seared
    Sea Scallops. 94

P

Pancakes, Cherry 22, *71*
Parmesan Pork Tenderloin
    with Red Onion Confit 103
Peppermint Cheesecake 117
Pies
    Door County Cherry . . . *76*, 108
    French Silk 110
    Montmorency Cherry
        Almond 109
Pilgrim Sandwich 79
Pineapple Salsa 85
Poppy Seed Torte. 120
Pork Tenderloin, Parmesan
    with Red Onion Confit 103
Poulet Asperge with Creamed
    Brandy Cider Sauce. 101

Q

Quiche, Crab, Artichoke Heart
    and Cream Cheese 30
Quiche, French Canadian 29

R

Raspberry Chicken
    Amandine *75*, 100
Raspberry Vinaigrette
    Dressing 56
Red Bell Pepper Bisque 44
Rhubarb Torte. 127
Rice
    Pudding, Breakfast 24
    Salad, Crabmeat and
        Wild. 63, *73*
    Salad, Curried Chicken 65
    Soup, Wild with Cream of
        Mushroom 42
Roasted Pecan Roquefort
    Dressing 58
Roasted Red Bell Pepper
    Sauce 87
Rolls, Candlelight Dinner
    Tied 36
Rolls, Morning Cinnamon . . 32, *72*
Rosemary Baked Rack
    of Lamb. *74*, 104

S

SALADS & SIDE DISHES
    Broccoli Salad 66
    Crabmeat and Wild Rice
        Salad. 63, *73*
    Curried Chicken Rice Salad . . 65
    Grilled Chicken Salad with
        Honey Lime Dressing. . 62, *73*

INDEX

Tortellini Pesto Salad. 64
Vegetable Barley Salad. 67
White Gull Inn Coleslaw . . . 69
White Gull Inn Potato Salad. 68
Winter Squash Casserole. . . . 70
Salsa, Pineapple. 85
SANDWICHES
  Cucumber Dill Sauce 81
  Garden Sandwich with
    Cucumber Dill Sauce 80
  Honey Dijon Sauce 78
  Open Doorwich with
    Honey Dijon Sauce. . . . *73*, 78
  Pilgrim Sandwich 79
  Vegetable Burgers 82
Sauces
  Brandy Cream. 111
  Brandy, Creamed Cider 101
  Cucumber Dill 81
  Dijon Gravy 25
  Grand Marnier 129
  Hollandaise. 97
  Honey Dijon. 78
  Pepper, Red Bell Roasted . . . 87
  Pineapple 85
  Raspberry. 100, 114
Scallops in Puff Pastry
  with Roasted Red Bell
  Pepper Sauce. 86
Scones, Buckwheat with
  Smoked Salmon and
  Cream Cheese. 89
Scones, Maple Pecan
  with Maple Butter. 35
Shrimp and Artichoke
  Romano 93
SOUPS
  Award Winning 3-Bean
    Chicken Chili. 49
  Black Bean 46
  Burgundy Mushroom 43
  Chicken Almond. 50
  Cinnamon Croutons 53

Cream of Garlic and Onion . . 41
Cream of Mushroom
  with Wild Rice. 42
Cream of Winter Squash. . . . 45
Door County Chilled
  Cherry 52
Gazpacho 54
Hearty Beef Barley 40
Italian Vegetable 48
Red Bell Pepper Bisque. 44
Tomato Dill 47
Wisconsin Beer Cheese. 51
Spinach, Herbed Cakes 90
Squash, Winter Casserole 70
Steve's Swedish Limpa Bread. . . 38
Stuffed Tenderloin Filet. 105

T

Tomato Dill Soup 47
Tortellini Pesto Salad. 64
Torte
  Blackberry Custard 118
  Poppy Seed 120
  Rhubarb 127
  Truffle Trio *76*, 124
Truffle Trio Torte. *76*, 124
Turkey Hash Browns
  with Dijon Gravy 25

V

Vegetable Barley Salad. 67
Vegetable Burgers 82

W

Walleye, Wisconsin
  au Gratin. 95

INDEX

White Chocolate Cheesecake
with Raspberry Sauce 114
White Chocolate Coconut
Cake 112
Whitefish Oscar with
Hollandaise Sauce 96
Whitefish Parmesan 99
White Gull Inn Coleslaw 69
White Gull Inn Fish Boil 98
White Gull Inn Granola . . . 23, 72
White Gull Inn Potato Salad . . . 68
Winter Squash Casserole 70
Wisconsin Beer Cheese Soup . . . 51
Wisconsin Walleye au Gratin . . . 95